HELPING TEENAGERS
with ANGER &
LOW SELF-ESTEEM

HELPING TEENAGERS
with ANGER &
LOW SELF-ESTEEM

Edited by MARGOT SUNDERLAND

A HINTON HOUSE Therapeutic Resource

HINTON HOUSE

Worksheet illustrations by Nicky Armstrong – www.nickyarmstrong.com

This book can be used in conjunction with *Smasher* by Margot Sunderland, an illustrated storybook to help adolescents with anger and alienation.

Published by

Hinton House Publishers Ltd, Newman House, 4 High Street, Buckingham, MK18 1NT, UK
T +44 (0)1280 822557 F +44 (0) 560 3135274 E info@hintonpublishers.com

www.hintonpublishers.com

The right of Margot Sunderland to be identified as the editor of this work has been asserted by her in accordance with the Copyright, Designs and Patents Act 1988.

© 2012 Margot Sunderland

First published 2012
Reprinted 2013

British Library Cataloguing in Publication Data
A CIP catalogue record for this book is available from the British Library.

ISBN 978 1 906531 30 0

Printed and bound in the United Kingdom by Hobbs the Printers

Contents

Worksheets & Exercises

About the Editor

Dr Margot Sunderland is Director of Education and Training at The Centre for Child Mental Health London, Honorary Visiting Fellow at London Metropolitan University, and a Child Psychotherapist with over thirty years' experience of working with children and families. She is the author of more than twenty books in child mental health, which collectively have been translated into eighteen languages and published in 24 countries. Her internationally acclaimed book, *What Every Parent Needs to Know* won First Prize in the British Medical Association Medical Book awards 2007 (Popular Medicine section). The book has also been voted one of the top brain books of our time by The Dana Foundation. Her books which form the *Helping Children with Feelings* series (Speechmark) are used as key therapeutic tools by child professionals throughout the UK and abroad.

Dr Sunderland is also Co-Founding Director of the higher education college, The Institute for Arts in Therapy and Education which runs Masters degree courses and Diplomas in Adolescent Therapy, Child Counselling and Parent-Child Therapy. She undertakes many speaking engagements on her work in the UK and abroad.

About the Contributors

Louise Bartel works as an Adolescent Therapeutic Counsellor, currently practicing at a BESD school for boys in Hampshire. She has over ten years' experience of working in BESD schools, in a variety of roles, both in Social Care and Education. She holds a Psychology degree and has training and qualifications in Child Development, Anger Management and Counselling. She has also completed a Diploma in Adolescent Therapeutic Counselling at the Institute for Arts in Therapy & Education. Louise has introduced innovative practices to her current workplace, seeking to support young people in their development, particularly through times of emotional turbulence. She leads a team whose work focuses on the importance of relationship and longer term therapeutic interventions, through facilitating opportunities for young people to make decisions that may result in positive, lasting changes to their behaviour.

Louise has made presentations to national and regional conferences for the Social, Emotional and Behavioural Difficulties Association (SEBDA) and 'engage in their future' (formerly the National Association of BESD Schools).

Lynne Davis is a UKCP registered Psychotherapist and trainer, working extensively with children, adolescents and adults who have been severely traumatised both in the National Health Service and privately. She has worked in adolescent Mental Health services for over six years and prior to this worked with challenging behaviours at the Maudsley Hospital and Feltham Young Offenders Institution. She has a diploma in therapeutic counselling with adolescents awarded by the Institute for Arts in Therapy & Education. Using her experience and training Lynne works to support clients who are often high risk and vulnerable. She also provides training for local authority social workers, foster carers and adoptive parents around attachment, trauma and adolescents.

Alison Eldridge is a UKCP Registered Adult and Child Psychotherapist and Registered Nurse in Mental Health. She is Director of Options Child and Family Therapy Services in Middlesbrough, Cleveland and formerly a Specialist Nurse Psychotherapist working in Child and Family Mental Health (CAMHS). Alison has a wealth of experience ranging from working with parents and children to working with children in care settings, schools, NPSCC, Barnardos and Action for Children in the North East of England.

Alison draws upon her twenty-eight years' experience offering insights and examples to help parents, carers and teenagers to relate more effectively.

Tracy Godfroy is a qualified and highly experienced child psychotherapist who also trained in transactional analysis and group dynamics. She has over ten years' experience of working with highly traumatised children and young people and their families at Tumblewood Community. The therapeutic community is for young girls aged between 11 and 18 years who have survived backgrounds of severe trauma, abuse and neglect. She also specialises in group and individual therapy with young people who have experienced sexual exploitation and inter-familial sexual abuse. Within the therapeutic relationship she encourages the use of the arts to enable highly intense psychological material to be explored safely and effectively.

Dom Guard works as a psychotherapist with families, parents, adolescents and children in private practice. He has worked therapeutically in many settings including at Family Futures Consortium, within schools, with school-excluded children, as an expert witness and on the Teens and Toddlers project. He is also a supervisor and regularly teaches at the Institute for Arts in Therapy & Education. He is the author of ten published storybooks for children.

Louis Sydney is a qualified Child and Adult Psychotherapist and Somatic Experience Practitioner. He originally trained as a Cruse bereavement counsellor. He was involved with the Marchioness Disaster team and Bristol Cancer Centre. This prompted a long and continued interest in attachment, loss and bereavement issues. An experienced trainer on arts-based therapeutic interventions, attachment, trauma and loss in families he has worked for nearly a decade with traumatised children and young people who are fostered and adopted in the context of their family setting (Adoptionplus, ASART and Family Futures Consortium). Louis now works independently offering family therapy, parent-child therapy, individual child and young peopleís therapy. This involves providing facilitated contact for families and using contemporary arts media in life-story work.

Introduction

Margot Sunderland

What an amazing stage of life, with all its dramatic hormonal changes, which can turn a sweet little child into a teenager who knows her own mind, becomes her own person and finds her own direction. If all goes well, transition to adulthood means young people fully engage with their drive and creativity, discover their sexuality in the context of a loving relationship, and develop a far deeper level of social and emotional intelligence. But if things go wrong, they can find themselves living with crippling feelings of shame, anxiety or depression, low self-esteem, peer pressure, identity crises and relationship breakdown with family members and friends. As a consequence they can turn to alcohol and drugs to self-medicate, withdraw and avoid, and/or discharge all their pain and rage through violent and anti-social behaviour. Illustrative of this is a very shocking statistic 'Every 22 minutes in the UK, a teenager tries to kill themselves' (Institute for Public Policy Research 2006).

When teenagers are clearly troubled, this book can really help. It is full of practical ways to connect with young people who seem unreachable or lost in bitterness or hate. The experienced contributors offer tried-and-tested interventions (showing that ASBOs and prison are not an inevitable outcome), which will enable teenagers to move away from angry and anguished ways of being, to self-awareness, self-esteem and an ability to thrive.

This book will be of particular value to child professionals and to parents who have repeatedly experienced feelings of failure, hopelessness and far too much stress when working and living with teenagers. It aims to be a vital support in terms of doing something different, when the pull with troubled teenagers is to get angry with them, withdraw from them and feel completely impotent. The book will offer hope and inspiration coupled with tools and techniques of what to say and how to be, in order to break the all-too-common cycle of emotional pain leading to violence.

As the Institute of Public Policy Research states, 'Tragically for too many children the transition to adulthood is complex, messy and unsuccessful', but it really doesn't have to be this way. I am convinced, based on all the latest neuroscientific and psychological research, that society really doesn't have to suffer from the level of teenage violent crime, depression, suicide rates, teenage pregnancy and many other forms of youth disaffection that we see today, and have seen for years. But if things are to change, research shows that far more people are going to have to have far more thoughtful, reflective and therapeutic conversations with far more teenagers. This book is about empowering people to have those conversations.

The Contributors and What They Offer

The contributors to this book have all worked with troubled teenagers for years. They demonstrate how they have been able to reach young people via creative interventions and key conversations which have enabled them to change the direction of their lives. All the contributors have found their own individual ways of connecting with teenagers. In so doing, they all concur that we must look further than a teenager's presenting angry, defensive or monosyllabic behaviour to their underlying painful feelings. These often include lack of self-confidence, self-hate, feeling unwanted, unappreciated, let down and having chronic low self- esteem as well as a whole host of unprocessed feelings about shocks, trauma and losses suffered in their childhood years.

The contributors discuss how aggressive teenage behaviour is often a communication of distress, which needs to be understood and addressed by an empathic adult. They discuss 'what to say and how to be' in terms of enabling teenagers to feel understand rather than blamed or shamed. Each contributor offers moving case studies and examples to bring their theory and practice to life. The book also includes key parenting skills, designed to empower both parents and professionals supporting parents, to ride out the inevitable emotional turbulence of this developmental stage with skill and grace, while keeping their own stress levels down at the same time!

The Worksheets: Vital Tools to Help Start Difficult but Essential Conversations with Teenagers

For so many adults the pull is to talk *at* the teenager rather than to listen *to* the teenager and to find ways for *them* to talk. The worksheets included in this book address the key feelings and issues common to teenage angst and torment. If these are not talked about, the teenager often discharges their emotional tension in primitive fight, flight or freeze behaviour. Sometimes the consequences of this have long-term adverse effects on their quality of life. Furthermore, adults often feel clumsy and inept when trying to start important conversations with troubled teenagers. The worksheets will enable adults to be with teenagers in confident, non-embarrassing and effective ways, so that the conversation flows rather than flounders.

The worksheets have been tried and tested with teenagers over several years and developed in conjunction with the teenagers themselves. They are straightforward and interesting to complete, and are designed to enable teenagers to safely and effectively address their true feelings lying beneath the defences, bravado, cold silences and aggression, in order that these feelings can be understood and resolved. Furthermore, the worksheets, all informed by psychology, will engender the teenager's interest and curiosity in themselves, their inner world and the human condition in general. They will be helped to understand why they do what they do and feel what they feel in a way that enables them to reflect on the support they need. In short, the worksheets demand very little from the defensive teenager and give a great deal.

This book can be used in conjunction with *Smasher* by Margot Sunderland, an illustrated storybook to help adolescents with anger and alienation.

Parent–Teenager Relationships: How to Get Them Right

Margot Sunderland

Adolescence is a time when intense emotions in the parent-teenager relationship are inevitable, so it is vital that parents receive support and information about how to manage them well. Research shows that how a teenager's emotional outbursts (not dissimilar to those of a toddler at times) are handled is a key factor in terms of whether this stage of development will be successful or not. More generally, the quality of parent–teenager relationships is a vital factor in determining whether a teenager will become clinically depressed, develop an anxiety disorder, move into anti-social behaviour or instead handle this developmental stage well. Research shows that arguments with parents and poor family relationships are a big deal to teenagers, even if on the surface they appear not to care.

The link between teenage mental-health problems and parent-teenager relationships is not surprising as the family is where we learn, or fail to learn, vital emotional and social skills for life: about relationships, skills for negotiation, relational repair, conflict resolution, empathy and compassion. But because teenagers are often rude, provocative, dismissing and abusive to parents, it is easy to see how negative patterns of relating are very common in parent-child relationships. In fact, responding effectively to an angry, sulky or violent teenager is a real art, requiring a lot of complex and sophisticated skills, which don't tend to come naturally.

This chapter offers key knowledge and interventions aimed at improving and harmonising parent-teenager relationships as a way of preventing mental ill-health in teenagers. If we continue to fail parents by not making sure they are empowered with these vital relational skills, we will continue to see the levels of youth crime and teenage mental ill-health that exist in our society today.

There are a huge number of research studies linking troubled family relationships with teenage mental ill-health and anti-social behaviour. Table 1 shows a summary of some this research.

TABLE 1: *Summary of Research Showing the Role of Parent-Teenager Relationships in Teenage Mental Health Issues*

Teenage Problem	Summary of Research
Internet addiction disorder	Teenagers who developed an internet addiction disorder consistently found their parents to be over-intrusive, punitive or lacking in emotional responsiveness (Lam et al 2009).
Obesity	In the 5–11 year-old age range, obesity was clearly linked to family stress, in particular due to lack of cognitive stimulation and emotional support in the household. In the 12–17 years age range, obesity was clearly linked to family stress, and in particular, to the mental and physical health problems and financial strain in the household (Garasky et al 2009).
Anti-social behaviour	When parents used verbal threats, swearing or hitting with the teenager, there was a clear connection with anger, anxiety, depression in the teenager (Peltonen et al 2010). When parents used smacking/hitting to discipline, there was an increased probability of anti-social behaviour in the teenager regardless of whether or not the rest of parenting was positive (Gámez-Guadix et al 2010). Anti-social behaviour was high in teenagers when high levels of conflict were reported in either parent-teenager or friendship relationships (Sentse & Laird 2010).
Risky behaviour (e.g., skipping school, sex, lying, drinking, stealing)	When parent-teenager relations were poor, the naturally elevated testosterone levels in adolescence were more likely to result in the teenager engaging in risky behaviour (e.g., skipping school, sex, lying, drinking and stealing). When parent-teenager relations were good the elevated testosterone levels didn't seem to matter and had no adverse effect on emotion or behaviour in the teenager! (Booth et al 2003)

Teenage Problem	Summary of Research
Depression	Negative family interactions served as a risk factor to teenage depression (Piko & Balazs 2010). Depressed mood was high when either parental or friendship support was low (Sentse & Laird 2010). Higher levels of parent-teenager conflict and poorer family functioning were associated with more depressive symptoms and headaches in teenagers (Lewandowski & Palermo 2009). Teenagers with depressed mothers experienced higher rates of anger, anxiety and depression, than teenagers whose mothers were not depressed. Mothers with a history of depression exhibited greater sadness during their interactions with their teenagers (Jaser et al 2008).
Self-harm	Teenagers who self-harmed had a poorer quality of attachment to both parents and higher levels of depression, anxiety and stress. Good attachment provides the teenager with stress regulation, so may be a maladaptive coping mechanism (Hallab & Covic 2010).
General psychological distress in teenagers	There were increases in self-reported psychological distress in teenagers due to arguments with parents, school disengagement, worry about school and, for girls, worry about family relationships (Sweeting et al 2010).
Teenage mental ill-health	When teenagers felt they couldn't talk to their parent about their problems and believed their parent didn't really care about them, there was an association with mental ill-health, unhealthy weight control, substance use, suicide attempts, body dissatisfaction, depression and low self-esteem (Ackard et al 2006).

Why are Parent-Teenager Relationships so Important in Terms of Whether or Not the Teenager is Troubled?

In answer to this, we must turn to neuroscience. A good relationship with, and secure attachment to, a parent means the teenage brain will activate optimal levels of opioids and oxytocin, not all the time of course (due to life's general stressors) but enough of the time to result in the teenager being mostly good natured. These biochemicals in the brain are anti-anxiety, anti-aggression chemicals (Panksepp 1998). In other words they protect the teenager from spending much of their time in angry, anxious or depressed moods fuelling negative interactions with their parent. We also know that when there has always been a good level of physical affection between parent and child, and this continues on some level into the teenage years (e.g., still having lots of cuddles), this again protects against teenage angst. This is due to physical affection activating oxytocin (see Panksepp 1998). Oxytocin sensitises the opioid system, making these anti-aggression molecules work even more effectively.

When parents are in conflict with their teenagers for a good deal of the time, the teenage brain will activate high levels of stress hormones instead of opioids and oxytocin. These all too easily trigger the teenager into feelings of anger, depression or anxiety.

In short, if we want to see a reduction in youth crime and teenage anti-social behaviour on our streets, we will need to improve parent-teenager relationships, because in so doing we will bring about a change to the habitual brain biochemical profile in the troubled teenager and activate their pro-social circuitries! Table 2 shows a summary of some of the research evidencing the positive outcomes from good parent-teenager relationships.

How Parents can Unwittingly Activate a Teenager's Stress Hormones, and Not their Anti-Anxiety, Anti-Aggression Brain Chemicals

In actuality, the ways that many parents relate to their teenagers means that they often unwittingly activate not those fabulous anti-aggression, anti-anxiety chemicals in the brain but instead toxic levels of stress chemicals. One of these stress chemicals is called CRF (cortico-releasing factor, a precursor to cortisol). When this chemical was pumped at high levels into the brains of mammals they became angry, anxious or depressed – all the very familiar ills of teenage angst!

TABLE 2: *Summary of Research Showing Why Good Parent-Teenager Relationships are a Major Factor in Teenage Health & Happiness*

Protection against youth offending, violence and other forms of anti-social behaviour.	On-going parental support is associated with lower offending in young adulthood (Johnson et al 2010). Teenage anti-social behaviour was low when either parent-child relationships or friendships were low in conflict (Sentse & Laird 2010). Teenagers were far less likely to move into anti-social behaviour when they enjoyed good, low-conflict relationships with their parents (Sentse & Laird 2010). Good parent-family relationships are protective against violence (Stoddard et al 2009).
Protection against teenage depression.	There was less teenage depression when parent support was high (Sentse & Laird 2010). Parental emotional responsiveness and authoritative parenting style is protective in terms of adolescent depression, particularly among girls (Pikó & Bálazs 2010).
Protection against the hormonal turbulence of the teenager years.	When parent-teenager relations were good, the naturally increased testosterone levels from this developmental stage had no adverse effect on emotion or behaviour in the teenager. When parent-teenager relations were poor, testosterone levels badly affected behaviour (Booth 2003).
Protection against aggressive personality where genetic vulnerability for higher negative reactions to stress exists.	Certain variants of the serotonin transporter gene 5-HTTLPR leave people with a genetic vulnerability to higher negative reactivity to stress. Insecurely attached teenagers who had this genetic vulnerability were rated as more aggressive. If the teenagers were securely attached, the genetic vulnerability didn't make any difference (Zimmermann et al 2009).
Protective for good problem-solving skills and good conflict resolution.	In the early-to-middle years adolescent group, positive problem-solving and conflict engagement spilled over from adolescent-parent relationships to adolescent friendships (Van Doorn et al 2011).

When parents get angry or irritated with their teenager, the reptilian part of the teenage brain often activates along with an alarm system in the amygdala, which is situated in the old mammalian part of the brain. As a result the more sophisticated parts of their brain (frontal lobes) are showered with excessively high levels of noradrenaline, cortisol, CRF and other stress hormones. When this happens, the teenager finds themselves overwhelmed by the primitive threat responses and totally unable to think in a rational or reasoned manner! They are likely to do one or more of the following:

✳ **FLIGHT** Run away, slam the door and go up to their bedroom or leave the house.

✳ **FIGHT** Be verbally abuse or aggressive – so we are now into a severe parent-teenager row.

✳ **FREEZE** Say nothing or shut down and sulk, become coldly silent etc., when parent tries to talk to them, which enrages the parent further.

All of this results in the misery outlined in the research described in Table 1 above.

In addition to this, teenagers get a bigger thrill hit (a higher level of the brain chemical dopamine) in their brains from exciting activities than adults. So if you are a teenager and you are a bit bored or under-stimulated, fighting with your mum and verbally abusing her can feel very exciting. You get a real psychological and brain chemical buzz. That said, as we have seen, the cost can be very high and the effects long-term. Research (see Table 1) shows that regular arguing and fighting can lead the teenager to believe that 'Mum doesn't like me'. This makes the whole world feel very insecure and can confirm the teenager's 'internal working models' (a concept devised by attachment theorist John Bowlby) of the self, others and life in general. Internal working models inform our moment-by-moment perception of the world.

Internalized working models of a teenager who feels disliked by his mum

✳ Internal working model of self: 'I am rubbish'

✳ Internal working model of other people: 'Other people are rubbish especially my mum.'

✳ Internal working model of life in general: 'Life stinks.'

It is not hard to see from this that the next step can be serious teenager depression.

Asking a teenager to simply finish the sentences:

✳ 'I am …'

✳ 'Other people are…'

✳ 'Life is…'

can be extremely informative in terms of the level of work you will need to put in to alleviate the teenager's suffering.

Key Parenting Skills to Help Activate a Teenager's Anti-Anxiety, Anti-Aggression Brain Chemicals instead of Stress Hormones

Skill One: Parents need to acknowledge their part in their teenager's problem.
The first skill is for parents to have the self-awareness and lack of defensiveness to accept that if their teenager is very troubled, their relationship will be playing a part (see research in Table 1).

The question then is how to make sure that the parent gets the support they need, e.g., to address their own depression, unworked-through trauma or loss, to be empowered with key parenting skills appropriate for teenagers, and to be enabled to have that important truth and listening conversation with their teenager (see more on this below).

Skill Two: Don't fall into the pattern of Teenager-Provocative-Action – Parent-Angry-Reaction.
We know that the parent and teenager will have a miserable time if they fall into the following very common pattern:

Teenager impulsive provocative action – Parent impulsive angry reaction

This is because such a pattern will activate stress hormones in both the parent's and teenager's brains and not the good anti-anxiety, anti-aggression chemicals. So instead we must look at how to support parents to replace this with:

Teenager impulsive provocative action – Thought-out intervention delivered calmly

Skill Three: When a parent wants to scream and shout at their teenager – think again! Try empathy instead (thought-out intervention delivered calmly).

As we have seen, when under stress, teenagers often move into primitive Fight, Flight, Freeze reactions. The pull is then for the adult to respond to them from the old mammalian/reptilian part of their own brain – to shout, scream, hit back with words in some way. But over time this can take a real toll on adult mental health (see Table 1). So it is best to do any screaming and shouting far away from the teenager, preferably in a different room with an empathic other present, who can provide emotional regulation. Having discharged all their pent-up energy, the adult is now able to greet the angry teenager from a place of calm and empathy.

Case Study – Wayne (age 16)

Wayne became very aggressive and depressed when his parents split up (see discussion of the effect of separation and divorce on teenagers in Chapter 2). He started to run away from home. On one occasion, after two nights away, he agrees to meet his mum in a park. On meeting up, his mum voices her anger.

Wayne's mum [impulsive angry reaction]: 'I've been worried sick about you – what do you think you were doing? You don't think of me, do you? You have no idea how worried I've been. You really are so selfish.'

Wayne listens and then walks off again [reptilian flight response]. His mum does not see him again for a further three nights.

Wayne's mum – alternative approach [thought-out intervention delivered calmly]: 'I am really sorry that since your Dad and I split up, home is not a place you want to be, but a place you want to run away from. I would really like to hear how you see things, why they feel so wrong for you. Then I can try to make things better for you. Perhaps we could go and have a cup of coffee somewhere now, as I really want to hear your side of things.'

Or put more simply:
'It seems that home is no longer a lovely place for you but is a painful place … Will you help me understand why that is so we can think of a way of changing things together?'

Case Study – Gemma (age 15)

Gemma has low self-esteem, is depressed and often shouts at her mum. One morning she gets up and can't find her shoes.

Gemma: 'Mum, you've moved my stuff again. You make my life so hard. You don't get it that I have to get out on time otherwise my friends don't wait…I hate you! You're useless!'

Gemma's mum [impulsive angry reaction]: 'How dare you talk to me like that! After all I've done for you. And you are a liar too! You know you lose your things, but you just can't face the fact that you only have yourself to blame, so you blame other people for your failings. You won't succeed in life if you keep doing that, you know!'

Gemma: 'I hate you!' Slams the door so hard a pane of glass falls out.

Gemma's mum – alternative approach [thought-out intervention delivered calmly]: 'So, life's pretty hard for you right now isn't it?'

Gemma: Bursts into tears and lets her mum hold her.

Skill Four: Don't take it personally.

There is absolutely no point in a parent taking a teenager's verbal attacks personally. Teenagers are genetically programmed to go off their parents at this developmental stage, and to attach to peers. If they didn't, they would never leave home! Even so, a lot of the insults aimed at parents are actually what they hate about themselves. So if teenagers accuse their parent of being useless, pathetic, weak, etc., it is often what they feel about themselves. The best approach is to use a key technique taken from psychotherapy. It is called empathising with the negative transference. This means the parent empathises with how the teenager is experiencing them at that moment and what it must feel like being the teenager when they are seeing the parent in such negative terms. They could start a sentence:

'So, you are seeing me as … and that must make you feel….'

Or:

'So, you are experiencing me as … and that must feel …'

Case Study – Tracey (age 13)

Tracey often thinks of herself as useless at schoolwork and feels pretty down about it.

Tracey: 'You just don't get it mum, do you? You nag, nag, nag, but you never really listen. You just talk at me all the time. You are a useless mum. I wish I had a better one. Actually, I don't even know if I am your child. I've often felt that I'm adopted and you just haven't told me.'

Tracey's mum [thought-out intervention delivered calmly]: 'So, you see me as someone who isn't interested in what you feel and think, and just wants to get you to listen to me and my criticisms. That must make you feel that you can't get through to me, that you can't get me to understand. And that I see what you do wrong, but don't appreciate what you do well. If this is how you see me, it must be frustrating, lonely and hurtful to be with me.'

Please note. If Tracey had sworn at her mum or called her names, that is verbal abuse. So as well as the empathy there must be consequences for this behaviour (see below, Skill Nine).

Skill Five: Because of what is happening in terms of brain development, it's likely that teenagers are going to mess up and sometimes in a big way. When they do, the parent needs to be a 'truth listener' and not a 'lie invitee'.

The therapist Ellyn Bader (2001) formulated the concept of 'truth listener and lie invitee'. Parents who are *lie invitees* react to a teenager's often shocking news about how they have messed up ('big time!') with impulsive feelings. They react by crying and/or by lashing out with anger. As a result, the teenager makes the decision (often with conscious awareness) never to go for help to their parents again with their fears, worries or problems. The teenager thinks 'Wow, if this is how mum reacts when I've messed up, then next time I'll simply lie to her'.

This is because their parent's response has made them feel worse and not better and they are likely to be feeling pretty awful anyway in terms of having messed up. They may even decide to have only bland, safe feelings from now on.

When you know that telling your parent about something you've messed up is going to result in outbursts of anger, of course the temptation is to lie. It is human to want a quiet life, but the resulting lack of authenticity, lack of real intimacy and real connectedness in the parent- teenage relationship can cost the teenager dearly (See Table 1).

When a parent can listen to shocking news from a teenager without flying into an angry critical attack or breaking down, this is a good relational skill. Instead of anger they are managing their emotional dysregulation and stress levels. They are aware that if they fly off the handle at the news, they could be written off by the teenager as a *lie invitee*. So when the teenager announces that they are pregnant or have been charged with shoplifting or are down at the police station, drunk and disorderly, the parent keeps their cool. The teenager then experiences them as a *truth listener*. They think 'Wow, mum was so good over that. I will definitely ask for her help if I mess up again and I'll tell her about my problem with that bully at school.'

A 'truth listening' parent may say something along the lines of 'Well, that is a shock. OK, I need to take in what you are saying. Let me think for a while about what might be the best course of action.' They then do just that. Once the situation has been addressed appropriately, the parent talks to the teenager about how they can support themselves to make better choices, and not more bad choices, in the future.

Statistics show that most troubled teenagers will not go to their mum or dad and ask for help or share their feelings and problems. Many parents are being 'lie invitees', without knowing the cost of this to their relationship with their teenager.

Skill Six: Using praise as protection against teenager troubles.
When parent-teenager relationships have become stressful and miserable for both parties, it is likely that a key contributory factor is lack of sufficient praise and reward. These are not just a nice extra, but essential in terms of activating the anti-anxiety, anti-aggression chemicals in the brain, and in so doing, deactivating the destructive stress hormones which so easily trigger aggression, anxiety or depression.

Sue Jenner (1999) found that if children and teenagers are going to thrive, parents must give at least six instances of praise or warm physical affection for every one criticism or command. If the reality is the reverse, or even worse, this can lead into the territory of the unwitting activation of stress hormones and mental ill-health.

It can be great to text praise and appreciation, or leave little notes under the teenager's pillow or by their cereal bowl – particularly if direct communication ends up with them saying 'Oh, you're just saying that mum'.

Howard Glasser's research (2006) on acknowledging the smallest 'moment of success' in a teenager has had dramatic results. He has turned whole school cultures around with this one technique. An example of noticing a moment of success would be as follows. Instead of walking past your teenager who is at last quietly playing on the internet, and thinking 'Phew, some peace at last', you could say 'Hey Simon, you are great at that game – what a score!'. Or instead of just being relieved that your teenager doesn't smoke you could say 'What a really intelligent thing you do by not smoking'.

Try to make a really big deal of acts of kindness, acts of negotiation and finding compromises.

Skill Seven: Rewards for a behaviour you want to change.
Charlie Taylor, author of *Divas & Doorslammers* (2010) outlines the power of using rewards for a specific behaviour you want to change. He acknowledges that just nagging the teenager to tidy their bedroom or to speak to their parents politely can have as much effect as whistling in the wind.

He suggests using monetary tokens of different value (from values as small as 10p onwards). Here are some of his excellent key points on use of rewards:

✳ Rewards help teenagers get back on track in the short term.

✳ Rewards should be used to change one specific behaviour at a time.

✳ They should be small, cheap and easy to administer. Don't be afraid to give out lots at first. Your teenager has to see quickly what's in it for him.

✳ Reward as soon as possible after the good behaviour.

✳ Rewards that offer a fantastic prize in the distant future (e.g., an iPod) seem alluring, but they are too remote to effect the day-to-day behaviour of children.

✳ One father said, 'If you are polite for a week I'll take you to a football match'. His son never achieved it. It is essential that the reward is attainable and that the teenager receives it regularly.

✳ If you create a reward system and the teenager is not earning rewards then you have set the bar too high and you are expecting too much.

Rewards can be used as a way of learning about the world of work as opposed to the view some teenagers have of 'My five-star hotel with Mum as slave'. They need to learn about the work ethic and also about the pleasure of earning. Pocket money is a great way of doing this while also using it as part of an on-going system of praise and rewards. You might for example, give a fifteen-year-old £15 a week, but with £5 of it dependent on them tidying their bedroom and £5 dependent on them helping prepare or clear away meals. Then they can earn more (like a bonus) if they do things like clean the windows, the car or do the washing. Tokens are a great idea, these can be cashed in for actual money perhaps once or twice a week. Tokens can also be lost through breaking one of the house rules (see below).

Skill Eight: The importance of house rules and having clear consequences for breaking them.

People often mistakenly think that house rules are just for younger children and not for teenagers. Arguably, they are even more important in the teenage years. Using house rules means making sure you carry out the consequences for breaking those rules.

Sample house rules for teenagers

✸ No television or computer until you've finished your homework, tided your room etc.

✸ No texting, phoning, computer games at family meal times (consequence – confiscation).

✸ Siblings. If you are fighting over the use of the internet or games console then the item will be taken away until you manage to think up a way to time share. If you need my help to work it out just ask.

✸ Verbal abuse of siblings. (This can be very serious as it has been shown to have an effect on brain development, Teicher et al 2010.) All pocket money will be taken for the week and you will need to do something helpful for the sibling. Family meetings will be called if it is felt that resentments need to be voiced, so this can be done in a structured, safe way and not a destructive, brain-damaging way. (See below, Skill Ten, for more on Family Meetings.)

Skill Nine: Give choices and consequences for unacceptable behaviour, because punishments on their own don't work.

> Punishments alone won't change bad behaviour. Make it clear to the child what you want him to do, then praise, and if necessary reward him.
>
> *(Taylor 2010)*

Punishments on their own (without rewards, praise, choices and consequences) don't work because they:

✳ Activate the brain's stress hormones and not the brain's pro-social systems.

✳ Make the negative relationship with the parent more negative, leading to increased alienation and often inspiring fantasies of revenge.

✳ Often have a higher cost for the parent than the teenager, e.g., 'Right, you are grounded for a month!' How awful for the parent to have an angry teenager in the house for all that time!

✳ Parent often can't stick to what they threaten, 'OK, you're not coming on holiday with us', so the teenager thinks the parent is a push-over and that the buzz of anti-social behaviour is worth it, as threats are not followed through.

✳ If a parent seems to be punishing and criticising the teenager for much of their time together, something has gone badly wrong. It usually points to a desert in terms of praise, appreciation, rewards and conversations aimed at resolving problems (see Family Meetings).

> When teenagers are misbehaving, punishments can make parents feel strong and powerful but the short-term control they gain at these moments can end up feeding into the pattern that makes the child misbehave.
>
> *(Taylor 2010)*

'Choices and consequences' is a phrase devised by Foster Cline (2006), one of the first practitioners to realise that if you are to socialise a teenager effectively, you need to take parental emotion out of the picture and address any negative behaviour in a calm tone relating simply what is to be done. This is because parental emotion stirs up negative emotion in the teenager and so is actually counterproductive to the task in hand. Talk in the language of choices and consequences.

> ## Case Study
>
> **Parent to teenager:** 'It's a shame you made that bad choice to call your brother an f-ing liar, because as you know swearing can be very damaging and so regrettably that means no pocket money this week.'
>
> **Parent to teenager:** 'Simon, I know you have taken money from my purse. That is a shame, because it was a bad choice and not one that I can let go by without a consequence. I am thinking about what a suitable consequence will be. I'll let you know when I have decided. I hope you make a better choice next time. In fact, just to let you know, a good choice would have been to discuss with me your need for money and we could have worked out a way for you to earn it.'

This factual non-shaming language helps the teenager to do a cost- benefit analysis in his head, perhaps: 'OK, yes, taking money from mum's purse hasn't paid off. She found out – so I feel ashamed about it and now there is a consequence. I guess she's right – I'll just ask her for the money next time'.

If the parent had not used the language of choices and consequences but rather erupted into anger and shaming accusations (e.g., 'You're a thief!') the teenager would be so flooded with stress hormones that he would have responded with flight, fight or freeze.

Please note: If you think the stealing has a deeper, underlying psychological cause then you may need to obtain professional help (see below).

When selecting an appropriate consequence it is important that the parents give themselves time to think. This is very different from just handing out punishments impulsively from a place of anger. Instead you could say, 'I feel angry about what has happened. [Here voicing an emotion, but not in a shaming or angry way.] I will let you know what I am going to do about it when I have had time to think about the whole thing.'

Common consequences for teenagers are: grounding, taking away pocket money (but only if they have no other sources of money, otherwise this doesn't hurt them), banning television, computer or games console use. Household chores can also be used to earn back confiscated items, but they must be really well done and require real effort and not just a quick five minutes, e.g. cleaning the kitchen.

Choices and consequences with extreme teenage behaviour

In the case of parent abuse (teenager abusing adults) you can also use choices and consequences. Again, in such circumstances, take the emotion out of the situation. As a result, the teenager will be far more likely to use their higher thinking brain and really take in what is being said, rather than triggering a response from the reptilian fight, flight, freeze brain.

Case Study – Toby (age14)

Toby had threatened his mother with a knife four times. He had hit his brother so hard across the head that he had needed three stitches and had also stabbed him in the leg on two occasions. He had broken five doors. His parents had gone to parenting classes and Toby had been given some CBT therapy but nothing was working. The police had been called three times, as Toby's mother was worried that he was going to carry through a threat to injure her new partner. Essentially, the family was living in abject fear. One day Toby's mother decided to use choices and consequences.

Toby's mum: 'Hi Toby, good to see you back from school. We have been thinking about how things are going, so we want to talk to you. Is that OK? Let's go to the café at the end of the road, I think it will be easier to have a good conversation outside of the house.' [They do so.]

'OK, as you know, we have a problem. We want to feel safe in our own home but each time you pick up a knife, hurt Billy or do things that hurt or destroy, we don't feel safe. We love you very much, but we don't actually want to live like this anymore. So you have a choice. We would love you to stay with us, but if you do, there would need to be no more knife threats, injury or damage to the property. If that feels like something you can't do, or don't want to agree to, we will need to make you and us safe by ringing up social services to organise some time apart. They will place you in a boarding school or residential home. Do you have any reaction to what we are saying?'

It is important not to forget that of course good choices must also be praised. One parent for example, texted her fifteen year with 'Great choice Sam for not taking drugs that evening like your mates'.

Skill Ten: Modelling good conflict resolution – Family Meetings.

Family meetings are a great resource, particularly when a negative pattern is becoming established between parent and teenager or teenager and sibling.

We know that without good conflict resolution skills, life is going to be difficult for any one! So family meetings that are handled well are a real gift for teenagers. It has been shown that one in two children will experience parental separation or divorce before the age of 16 (Benson 2010). Many of these breakdowns are due in part, to an absence of conflict resolution skills. In family meetings feelings are thought about rather than just discharged. This is in line with brain research which shows that putting very strong feelings into words will calm the brain's alarm systems (Hariri et al 2000).

Family meetings should involve structured exercises, which make voicing your own resentments and hearing those of other people far easier.

The stages of a good family meeting

✹ Call a meeting – explain the rules.

✹ The Golden Rule – no talking at the same time as someone else.

✹ Say something along the lines of: 'First we will hear from x, then from y. I will ask you what you are angry about. I will write down what you say so I can really understand it. I will then say it back to you, to make sure I have really understood.'

✹ Listen to, and write down, the teenager's feelings and concerns.

✹ Read back to the teenager what you have written down, but include empathy.

Case Study

'So, Dan, you want to play War Hammer on the internet for a longer time because it spoils your fun just to do it for 30 minutes. And you feel very cross when you've just set something up and then Bill comes along and says it's his turn. I can see how frustrating that is, and understand why you want to discuss the sharing time limits in a meeting. Having to share something you really like can be painful.'

✹ Repeat the process with all the other children and teenagers in the house.

✹ Ask all members of the family to write down their solution to the problem.

✹ Ask all members of the family to read out their solutions to the problem.

✹ Decide which solutions you can all live with. You might want to use one solution one week and another the next.

✹ Next week review how things have gone.

Skill Eleven: Know when teenage behaviour or troubled mood points to a deeper underlying problem: unprocessed trauma or loss

If troubled teenage behaviour persists, or there is a really entrenched depression or anxiety problem, e.g., a phobia or obsession, or violent behaviour this may well be due to an unresolved trauma or loss. The tell-tale symptom of post-traumatic stress disorder is re-victimisation. This is where a teenager's behaviour involves some shocking cruelty but the teenager seems to be emotionally cut off from what they are doing.

The teenager will be doing to another some version of what they have experienced or witnessed (the latter commonly being domestic violence.) As Freud said in 1909, 'A thing which has not been understood inevitably reappears; like an unlaid ghost it cannot rest until the mystery has been solved and the spell is broken'.

The skill here is to know when a behaviour transcends common teenage troubles and reaches an extreme point of self-abuse or abuse of others. Then the urgent need is to refer on to a trained psychologist.

Bibliography

Ackard D.M., Neumark-Sztainer D., Perry C. & Story M. (2006) 'Parent-Child Connectedness and Behavioral and Emotional Health Among Adolescents', *Am J Preventative Med.* 2006 Vol. 30(1): 59–66.

Almendros C., Carrobles J.A., Gámez-Guadix M., Muñoz-Rivas M.J. & Straus M.A. (2010) 'Corporal punishment and long-term behaviour problems: the moderating role of positive parenting and psychological aggression.' *Eur Child Adolesc Psychiatry* Vol. 19(11): 813–22. Epub 2010 Sept 7.

Anderson C.M., Andersen S.L., Kim D.M., Teicher M.H., Navalta C.P. & Polcari A. (2003) 'The neurobiological consequences of early stress and childhood maltreatment', *Neuroscience and Biobehavioral Reviews* Jan-Mar Vol. 27(1–2): 33–44.

Asgeirsdottir B.B., Gudjonsson G.H., Sigfusdottir I.D. & Sigurdsson J.F. (2011) 'Physical activity buffers the effects of family conflict on depressed mood: A study on adolescent girls and boys.' *J Adolesc.*

Bader E., Pearson P. & Schwartz J. (2001) *Tell Me No Lies: How to Stop Lying to Your Partner – And Yourself – In the 4 Stages of Marriage*, Sunlight Press, New York.

Balázs M.A. & Pikó B. (2010) 'Control or involvement? Relationship between parenting style and adolescent depression', *Psychiatr Hung.* Vol. 25(6): 538–544.

Baur L.A., Hardy L.L., Hattersley LA., Howlett S.A., King L.A. & Shrewsbury V.A. (2010) *Physical Activity Nutrition Obesity Research Group*, University of Sydney, Australia.

Benson H. (2010) 'Family breakdown is not about divorce', Centre for Social Justice and Bristol Community Family Trust, Westminster London.

Bookheimer S.Y., Harir A.R. & Mazziotta J.C. (2000), 'Talking about feelings 'Modulating emotional responses: effects of a neocortical network on the limbic system', *Neuroreport* Jan; Vol. 1(17): 43–48.

Booth A., Johnson D.R., Granger D.A., Crouter A.C. & McHale S. (2003) 'Testosterone and Child and Adolescent Adjustment: The Moderating Role of Parent–Child Relationships', *Developmental Psychology* Vol. 39(1): 85–98.

Centre for Social Justice (2011) 'Mental Health: Poverty, Ethnicity, and Family Breakdown', Interim Policy Briefing, Westminster, London.

Cline F. & Fay J. (2006) *Parenting Teens with Love and Logic* NavPress; Upd Exp edition.

Compas B.E., Champion J.E., Fear J.M., Jaser S.S., Reeslund K.L. & Reising M.M. (2008) 'Maternal sadness and adolescents' responses to stress in offspring of mothers with and without a history of depression', *Adolesc Psychol.* Oct; Vol. 37(4): 736–46.

Der G., Sweeting H., West P. & Young R. (2010) 'Can we explain increases in young people's psychological distress over time', *Soc Sci Med.* Nov; Vol. 71(10): 1819–30. Epub 2010 Sep

Eisenmann J.C., Garasky S., Gundersen C., Lohman B.J. & Stewart S.D. (2009) 'Family stressors and child obesity', *Soc Sci Res.* Dec; Vol. 38(4): 755–66.

Ellonen N., Helweg-Larsen K., Larsen H.B. & Peltonen K. (2010), 'Parental violence and adolescent mental health', *Eur Child Adolesc Psychiatry* Nov; Vol. 19(11): 813–22. Epub 2010 Sept. 7.

Feldman R. (2010) 'The relational basis of adolescent adjustment: trajectories of mother-child interactive behaviours from infancy to adolescence shape adolescents' adaptation', *Attach Hum Dev.* Jan; Vol. 12(1–2): 173–92.

Gámez-Guadix M., Straus M.A., Carrobles J.A., Muñoz-Rivas M.J. & Almendros C. (2010) 'Corporal punishment and long-term behavior problems: the moderating role of positive parenting and psychological aggression', *Psicothema* Nov; Vol.22(4): 529–36.

Garasky S., Stewart S.D., Gundersen C., Lohman B.J. & Eisenmann J.C. (2009) 'Family stressors and child obesity', *Soc Sci Res.* Dec; Vol. 38(4): 755–66.

Giordano P.C., Johnson W.L., Manning W.D. & Longmore M.A. (2010). 'Parent-Child Relations and Offending During Young Adulthood', *J Youth Adolesc.*

Glasser H. & Easley J. (2006) *Transforming the Difficult Child*, Worth Publishing, London.

Goossens F.A., Koot H.M., Schuengel C. & Willemen A.M. (2008) 'Physiological reactivity to stress and parental support: comparison of clinical and non-clinical adolescents', *Clin Psychol Psychother* Sep; Vol. 15(5): 340–51.

Hallab L. & Covic T. (2010) 'Deliberate self- harm. The interplay between attachment and stress', *Behaviour Change* Vol. 27(2).

Hariri A.R., Bookheimer S.Y. & Mazziotta J.C. (2000) 'Modulating emotional responses: effects of a neocortical network on the limbic system', *Neuroreport* Jan. 17; Vol. 11(1): 43–8.

Henriksen T.B., Linnet K.M., Obel C., Slemming K., Sørensen M.J. & Thomsen P.H. (2010) 'The association between preschool behavioural problems and internalizing difficulties at age 10–12 years', *Eur Child Adolesc Psychiatry* Oct; Vol. 19(10): 787–95.

Jaser S.S., Fear J.M., Reeslund K.L., Champion J.E., Reising M.M., Compas B.E. (2008) 'Maternal sadness and adolescents' responses to stress in offspring of mothers with and without a history of depression', *Adolesc Psychol.* Oct; Vol. 37(4): 736–46.

Jenner S. (1999) *The parent-child game*, London: Bloomsbury

Jessop J. & Ribbens McCarthy J. (2005), *The impact of bereavement and loss on young people*, Joseph Rowntree Foundation.

Laird R.D. & Sentse M. (2010) 'Parent-child relationships and dyadic friendship experiences as predictors of behavior problems in early adolescence', *J Clin Child Adolesc Psychol.* Nov; Vol.39(6): 873–84.

Lam L.T., Peng Z.W., Mai J.C. & Jing J. (2009) 'Factors associated with Internet addiction among adolescents', *Cyberpsychol Behav.* Oct; Vol. 12(5): 551–55.

Lewandowski A.S. & Palermo T.M. (2009). 'Parent-teen interactions as predictors of depressive symptoms in adolescents with headache', *Psychol Med Settings*, Aug 13. Dec; Vol. 16(4): 331–8.

McAlaney J., McCambridge J. & Rowe R. (2011) 'Adult consequences of late adolescent alcohol consumption: a systematic review of cohort studies', *PLoS Med.* Feb 8; 8(2): e1000413.

Mohr C., Spangler G. & Zimmermann, P. (2009) 'Genetic and attachment influences on adolescents' regulation of autonomy and aggressiveness', *J Child Psychol Psychiatry*; Epub 2009 Sep 21. Nov; 50(11): 1339–47

Panksepp J. (1998) *Affective Neuroscience: The Foundations of Human and Animal Emotions*, Oxford University Press, Oxford.

Peltonen K., Ellonen N., Larsen H.B. & Helweg-Larsen K. (2010) 'Parental violence and adolescent mental health', *Eur Child Adolesc Psychiatry.* Nov; Vol. 19(11): 813–22. Epub 2010 Sep 7.

Pikó B. & Balázs M.A. (2010) 'Control or involvement? Relationship between parenting style and adolescent depression', *J Am Acad Psychoanal Dyn Psychiatry* Fall; Vol. 38(3): 503–31.

Ploegmakers-Burg M. & Stortelder F. (2010) 'Adolescence and the reorganization of infant development: a neuro-psychoanalytic model', *J Am Acad Psychoanal Dyn Psychiatry* Fall Vol. 38(3): 503–31.

Pryor J. & Rogers B. (1998) *Divorce and separation: The outcomes for children*, Joseph Rowntree.

Sentse M. & Laird R.D. (2010) 'Parent-child relationships and dyadic friendship experiences as predictors of behavior problems in early adolescence', *J Clin Child Adolesc Psychol.* Nov; Vol. 39(6): 873–84.

Sieving R.E., Stoddard S.A. & McMorris B.J. (2010) 'Do Social Connections and Hope Matter in Predicting Early Adolescent Violence?' *Am J Community Psychol.* Dec 23.

Stoddard S.A., McMorris B.J. & Sieving R.E. (2009) 'Do social connections and hope matter in predicting early adolescent violence?', *Am J Community Psychol.* Dec; Vol. 48(3-4): 247–56.

Sweeting H., West P., Young R. & Der G. (2010) 'Can we explain increases in young people's psychological distress over time?' *Soc Sci Med.* Nov; Vol. 71(10): 1819–30. Epub 2010 Sep.

Taylor C. (2010) *Divas & Door Slammers: The Secret to Having a Better Behaved Teenager*, Vermilion, London.

Teicher M.H., McGreenery C.E., Polcari A. & Samson J.A., (2006) 'Sticks, stones, and hurtful words: relative effects of various forms of childhood maltreatment', *The American Journal of Psychiatry.* Jun; Vol. 163(6): 993–1000.

Teicher M.H., McGreenery C.E., Polcari A., Samson J.A. & Sheu Y.S. (2010) 'Hurtful words: association of exposure to peer verbal abuse with elevated psychiatric symptom scores and corpus callosum abnormalities', *The American Journal of Psychiatry.* (12): 1464–71. Epub 2010 Jul 15. Dec; 167.

Van der Kolk B.A. (2003) The neurobiology of childhood trauma and abuse', *Child and adolescent psychiatric clinics of North America* 12: 293–31.

Van Doorn M.D., Branje S.J., Vandervalk I.E., De Goede I.H. & Meeus W.H. (2011) 'Longitudinal spillover effects of conflict resolution styles between adolescent-parent relationships and adolescent friendships', *J Fam Psychol.* Feb; Vol. 25(1): 157–61.

Weisskirch R.S. (2011) 'No Crossed Wires: Cell Phone Communication in Parent-Adolescent Relationships', *Cyberpsychol Behav Soc Netw.* Jan 4.

Winnicott D.W. (1971) *Playing and Reality*, Tavistock Publications Ltd, London.

Zimmermann P., Mohr C. & Spangler G. (2009) 'Genetic and attachment influences on adolescents' regulation of autonomy and aggressiveness', *Journal of Child Psychological Psychiatry* Nov; Vol. 50(11): 1339–47.

Helping Troubled Teenagers: What Every Parent & Child Professional Needs to Know

Alison Eldridge

Understanding the challenges and needs of teenagers can be confusing for both parents or primary carers and the teenagers themselves. This chapter explains what happens in the brain of a teenager, why they need to defend themselves and their decisions by using anger. It also discusses the importance of boundary setting in order to uphold the process of separation and individuation throughout adolescence. Practical advice, drawing on experience of working with teenagers is offered to help both parents and teenagers to work together.

The Teenager's Struggle

Adolescence is a time of great change, of emerging responsibilities, of bodily changes and the 'beginning of the end' of our childhood. For the teenager, new-found responsibilities and decisions weigh heavily on their time, thoughts and energy. Until this point, tasks and responsibilities have been structured and supported by the adults surrounding them. The journey into independence creates high levels of anxiety and fear for parents and teenagers alike. Each teenager is expected to be able to do more; to take responsibility for the cleaning of their bedroom, to help with some of the housework, to arrive on time for lessons and to be in the right place with the right equipment. Their protests about these tasks being too much all at once are often met with laughter or sarcasm from adults, rather than a true understanding of the enormity of the task.

Throughout adolescence these age-appropriate tasks escalate and the teenager is driven to separate from their caregivers. When a teenager feels overwhelmed or ill equipped they experience high levels of anxiety. If parents allow them to talk and feel understood then they will find a way of working through this, and be supported. Failure to support them is likely to result in them holding on to anxiety and stress internally until it either leaks out, or explodes in another setting such as school. Angry behaviours can include bullying, breaking things, stealing, fighting and sexual promiscuity, to name just a few.

Heated discussions and arguments are daily events in the household as the teenager and their parents struggle with the balance of wanting or needing to separate, versus the fear of separating. This dilemma can often leave both parent and teenager feeling overwhelmed, unsure of how to manage this and low in confidence. Teenagers who do not feel safe enough to engage in the power struggle at home are likely to challenge in another setting.

Raging hormones, exacerbating each feeling to gigantic proportions, fuel the internal world of the teenager. It is essential that some of the negative spirals of anger and frustration are interrupted and challenged in a caring and sensitive way. Adolescents can teach us much about how our behaviour as adults affects the developing teenager's view of the world.

When the adults get the balance right, the teenager feels skilled and supported and is generally happy in their lives. When the teenager holds too little or too much power this often results in them feeling very unsafe, increasing the possibility of an eruption of dangerous, oppositional or defiant behaviour.

Understanding Brain Development in Adolescence

When a baby is born its brain is not completely formed. Over the first two or three years of the infant's life, the experiences they encounter forge pathways in the brain. As each experience is repeated, the pathways are strengthened until they become hard-wired and stored as ways of being and doing. They become the template of our learning, colouring our understanding of people and events in the world.

During adolescence the brain undergoes huge changes, with a major increase in synaptic connections in the frontal lobes and later a major pruning process. The teenage brain is flooded with hormones, which drive this process, a process that takes control of their bodies and brains simultaneously. Such major brain changes often lead to a downturn in the teenager's level of empathy. The once caring and helpful son or daughter refuses to help with small tasks around the house, and appears to lose any sense of empathy or sympathy for anyone else.

Case Study

Suzie displayed her lack of empathy towards her mother saying, 'Why do I need to help with the washing? That's your job!' believing her mother was being completely unreasonable. She often made comments to her mother such as, 'Stop giving all your jobs to me, you're the mum … if you didn't want kids, then you shouldn't have had them!'

Adolescents often seem selfish and self-centred. However, outside the home they may be very busy developing their skills of empathy with their peers or in the larger world. Boys appear to lose the ability to speak coherently and frequently absent themselves from being any part of the family unit. This is all normal development and will pass at the end of adolescence. For the teenager, non-essential care for others compromises their need to deal with their here-and-now tasks. Balancing their need to belong and to separate concurrently increases their confusion and frustration. Their experiences and brain growth can often leave them feeling very unsafe and out of control.

The hormonal changes in the brain drive the teenager to experience the world independently, testing their abilities to cope with overwhelming, and often dangerous situations. Young people who have experienced a solid foundation of care with warm and loving parents or carers are able to call upon these experiences. For those who have not established a template of caring, this can be a time when dangerous behaviours can have catastrophic effects. The experience of not feeling cared for can easily be interpreted as 'I am unlovable' or 'I don't matter'. Such internal negativity can create a lack of self-care or negative spiral of self-punishment. If adults fail to interrupt the teenager's internal process through putting the time in to have healing conversations with them, it can manifest in the creation of eating disorders, alcohol misuse, substance misuse, self-mutilation and sexually uninhibited or anti-social behaviours.

When the teenager does not feel safe, they may demonstrate their fear by projecting this out on the world. This is not a conscious process that is thought through, but more of demonstration of 'This is how it is done'.

Case Study – Julie (age 12)

Julie, aged 12, was found to be in a sexual relationship with a boy aged seventeen. Julie was spending her social time drinking alcohol with groups of older boys and girls. She was unable to understand her parent's concerns and was furious with them, telling me, 'I dunno what all the fuss is about, I'm just out with me mates! What do you expect me to do, stay in and watch the telly with HER [Mum]!' Julie's need to belong merged with her developing sexuality, creating a confusion of what to share, and what not to share, of herself.

The Parent's Struggle

For parents, the journey is not an easy one as each teenager challenges their parental rules, requests and expectations. Just as the teenager feels overwhelmed and out of control the process is paralleled in the parents' experience, as they watch their smiling, happy child become sullen, argumentative and more and more absent from the family. Just when the parents are beginning to carve their own lives and careers, a new, far more frightening world begins to emerge. One parent described her role as, 'a permanent policeman' as her daughter began using computer networks to communicate with the wider world.

The skill of effective parenting is to guide young people through their developmental journey, knowing when to step in but also knowing when to step back. Giving teenagers the tasks of independence in bite-size pieces, while being available to help them to work through the inevitable difficulties, enables them to feel supported to make decisions. The balance of parenting is not something that can necessarily be taught, we cannot create a definite right and wrong template; however there are some indicators to help us in the journey. Parents who have already managed this process with one child may have to develop a different pace, approach and level of support for subsequent children. One mother likened this process to 'learning a different language'.

Many struggling parents feel isolated by this experience, viewing it as a personal failure as they compete with other parents to produce the perfect child. Of course, there is no such thing as a perfect child and certainly no perfect teenager!

Many parents appear to keep their journey private from others, feeling it may reflect their failure as a parent. They tell other parents or friends only the good things their son or daughter has done, omitting the very difficult behaviours that are often present. It is important to accept that just as all developing teenagers struggle at this time, so too do the parents.

The Building Blocks of Who We Are

Painful life experiences interrupt the emotional, social and educational development of young people as their energy is diverted from attending to day-to-day events in order to understand and process their feelings about what is happening in their worlds. Situations such as a pet dying, one of their carers leaving or becoming ill, an accident involving them or another person close to them, are common interruptions. These are life events that cannot be avoided. However, for the child they can be a great shock, causing physical pain or emotional trauma. From the adult's viewpoint such interruptions may seem to have been dealt with without having an impact on the developing child. But in adolescence the fall-out is made manifest.

Children learn through the repetition of tasks. Each task is repeated over and over again so that it is finally hard-wired into the brain. When early lessons in how to do a particular task are interrupted, both the task and possible solutions remain incomplete. These gaps in early experiences can often go unnoticed by both the adults and child, particularly if they do not impinge on the here-and-now experiences.

Case Study

One girl told me 'I always feel left out in new situations … I usually stay on the outside and watch rather than be in on it'. After some exploration we discovered her early experience of learning how to socialise had been interrupted when at the age of four, her mother became ill and was taken into hospital. She had been preoccupied with the loss of her mother and had missed the important learning experience of *how* to meet and play with other children as she tackled the difficult task of attending school. She clarified this by telling me, 'It was like missing half a term of French'.

Understanding the Fluctuating Needs of the Teenager

The teenager senses the gaps in their how-to-do experiences and automatically attempts to fill them in. One mother describes this coming and going behaviour as follows, 'One minute she is asking me for make-up and the next she acts like a little kid, wanting me to entertain and amuse her!' The journey consists of acting age-appropriately one minute, then wanting to be little and looked-after the next. Parents need to respect, and give time and space to the teenager's need to regress as they yo-yo between being independent and dependent. Building blocks which are not complete draw the teenager back in an effort to complete them. I have met many twelve- and thirteen-year-old girls who need to play with dolls to re-live the experience of how to care and be cared for, and fourteen- to sixteen-year-old boys who need to battle between 'the goodies and the baddies' using toy soldiers.

Society sees the emerging adult in teenagers as they display their skills at successfully mastering complicated tasks. Expectations are made of the newly skilled teenager to act age-appropriately and responsibly, not taking into account their need to fluctuate back and forth in developmental tasks. For teenagers, the excitement and need for control in their own lives has to be balanced with their need to have guidance and support about what is, and what is not, acceptable and safe behaviour.

Balancing power and responsibility is a task that must be negotiated constantly for the developing teenager. Parents must achieve the same balance. How much the teenager is able to manage effectively, and what supervision or support they might need fluctuates from time to time as the boundary of power and control must be re-negotiated, and eventually moved from adult to teenager.

When Parental Boundaries are Too Weak

Teenagers who have been rewarded for controlling/demanding behaviour, or who have been given too few boundaries or too little guidance quickly find themselves in situations in which they feel overwhelmed or ill-equipped to cope. As they have not learned about negotiation or reflection, they tend to make very bad decisions. A parent or teenager who deliberately makes 'bad' decisions is a rarity. We all do the best we can with the skills and knowledge that we have. Unprepared or ill-equipped teenagers *will* make mistakes!

One boy explained, 'One minute I am out with my mates, and yeah we were drinking, the next someone is passing around speed … it's in front of all my mates so I can't say no!' And, as one teenage girl explained, 'I'm not gonna be the only one who hasn't got a boyfriend! God, I just wouldn't dare!' A teenager's need to be the same makes them very vulnerable to suggestions from both their peer group and from predatory adults as they strive to fit in and conform. The level of fear teenagers might experience is overridden by their need to fit in, so they join in, rather than experience what they may see as failure to belong or perceiving themselves as 'different'.

Parents and carers need to be able to say 'no' to the teenager when necessary, and offer a rationale explaining why. Asking questions about where they are going, what they are doing and who they will be with are necessary, despite the protests this questioning may cause. Parents need to pay attention to the teenager's relationships, showing interest and maintaining the dialogue between parent and teenager. In time, the teenager will give feedback, although it may take a year or two for this to happen. For example, 'I'm glad you didn't let me go to that party last year, it got really out of hand'. Groups of teenagers 'check out' their progress and the 'fairness' of the agreed boundaries with their friends. An example of this would be the boundary of bedtime. Accepting boundaries which differ slightly from those of their friends, models differing options for managing the same situation.

Making sure that the teenager has a mobile phone means that they can have the freedom to be independent and yet can summon help should it be needed. A mobile phone also ensures that parents can contact them should it be necessary. Boundaries of times and availability need to be negotiated. Once agreed they need to be held firmly by the adult. The role of the teenager is to stretch the boundaries, while the role of the adult is to hold the boundaries. A parent who changes or alters the boundary after it has been agreed suggests they do not mean what they say. If a teenager knows their parents mean what they say, then they become reliable and predictable. If they experience the opposite, they are highly likely to challenge all boundaries. Inconsistent boundaries can leave the teenager feeling unsafe, confused and alone. Of course, boundaries can be changed when the teenager feels more able to manage social tasks on their own. Experiencing the parent or carer's fixed boundary enables the teenager to create their own non-negotiable internal boundary, hard-wiring it within their brain. This then becomes the 'how-to-do guide' for subsequent situations.

Of course, adults can't always be there when the teenager is faced with new and dangerous situations. At times of danger the brain automatically triggers a primitive threat response, which is designed to help us to either fight or run away. This fight or flight response is the body's own alarm system which automatically alerts us to danger, allowing us to protect ourselves. Our bodies flood with adrenaline which raises the heart rate and prepares the body to run from danger if necessary. This hyper-aroused state is often experienced by the teenager as excitement. 'I tell you I was buzzin' … we took this guy's car, he nearly caught us, but we just pulled off in time … ha ha'.

Confronting the teenager's dangerous behaviour can be difficult for a parent or carer, but it is essential. In defence, the teenager fights off their own doubts and any external criticism by distancing themselves, belittling others' views, creating a 'one up' standpoint. A lack of loving confrontation however, means they will often blindly repeat the dangerous tasks, sometimes with awful consequences.

Beneath the defence of omnipotence the teenager often feels sad, lonely, unloved, and angry or rejected by their parents for not keeping them safe. In contrast, they often experience relationships with their peers as caring, supportive and even loving.

Not everything in life is negotiable, therefore a parents' permission needs to reflect this. The decision of what can be, and what definitely is not, up for negotiation stands firmly in the control of the parents. Some non-negotiable boundaries may include not giving permission for something a teenager wants to do 'now'! Activities that are driven by the 'do it now' principle are often high-risk situations. Maintaining this boundary does eventually calm the inevitable feelings of anger and frustration that may be experienced as a result. In time, even the non-negotiable boundaries may need to alter once new skills and abilities are acquired.

When Parental Boundaries are Too Tight

Young people who experience boundaries which are too tight are likely to escalate their behaviour using anger. Some parents struggle to allow their children to become independent, too strictly limiting the teenager's level of power and control in life situations. The teenager's chemically driven need to separate is then continually hindered by the parent's reluctance to allow them to do so. To make matters worse, the teenager may become very aware of being different from their peers and may be teased and taunted as a result. The frustration of the teenager builds up over time and can drive them to 'do it anyway' without adult guidance and support.

Those who manage to tolerate their parents' overprotection complete their adolescence ill-equipped for life. They are expected to manage situations they have never encountered or rehearsed without adult guidance. The fear and anxiety experienced can inhibit their desire to individuate from their parents and can place them in a higher level of danger.

Case Studies

One seventeen-year-old girl said, 'I thought he just wanted to kiss me, but he wouldn't stop. I got so scared I couldn't stop him … I giggle when I get nervous'.

A single mother avoided her own fear of being separate by encouraging her daughter to share her bed. As her daughter reached seventeen the mother met and married another man, resulting in her daughter being moved into her own bedroom. The daughter experienced this as a total rejection. Her feelings of abandonment prevented her from enjoying an age-appropriate sense of separation and independence.

Communicating with Teenagers and Managing Angry Outbursts

The key to effective parenting of the teenager is balance and negotiation. It is a gradual process that occurs as a result of working together. Both the teenager and parent need to be comfortable with its pace. A parent's role is to walk the journey alongside the teenager, allowing them to be independent and separate in a staged way. Communication in general is often far easier for the teenager to hear and act upon if it is made in third-person terms, rather than it being openly directed toward their behaviours. Direct questions and confrontations about the teenager's behaviour may be experienced by them as exposing and shameful and is likely to invite outbursts of hostility and aggression.

Watching the television programmes that interest the teenager is a very useful way of communicating. They will be drawn to storylines which mirror their own experiences. Paying attention to the programmes they watch, talking about the characters and the storylines, but above all being interested in what they think or believe are essential. If parents are open and non-critical in these discussions they are able to find out more about the dilemmas and the influences surrounding the teenager.

As the teenager experiences more life situations, they need to be able to recognise in themselves what triggers a major stress response: the flooding of adrenaline, butterflies in the stomach, shallow breathing, and racing heart. It is helpful to identify and name this process for the teenager, explaining that alarm systems in their body and brain have been triggered. Teaching them to stop and think at this point helps them to listen to their own body. Once they can stop and reflect, they can generate options for each situation, helping them to *think* rather than just act.

Case Study

One girl seemed unable to recognise when a situation became dangerous. After talking to her about her physical response she became much more aware of her own bodily reaction towards the threat in the situation. When I added an 'Aaarrrgh!' response to an imaginary dangerous situation together with a waving of my arms while running around the room, we laughed together.

Two weeks later, the girl reported that she had found herself in a compromising situation but had remembered the arm-waving response we had practised together, saying, 'I heard you shouting "Aaarrrgh!" in my head and could just see you running around the room'.

> Her memory of me was linked to her internal experience of fear, which helped her to recognise that she needed to stop and think about the situation rather than 'do it anyway'. If the teenager can understand that there are *many* options for any given situation it will help them to think and not just simply act or react.

To assist the relationship between the parent and teenager, I regularly suggest a pause button is used when they begin to lose contact with each other. Either party can activate it at any time. This may be simply a word or phrase such as 'Chill', 'Cool it!', 'Whoa!' or any cultural 'in' word. By allowing the teenager to stop the adults from discussing something further, they are given a share of the power in the relationship. If both parties can learn to recognise when they have lost contact with the other they have the opportunity to re-establish contact.

Practising Independence

Independent tasks outside the home need careful negotiation. The age at which a child can perform certain tasks alone is, of course, controversial. I would suggest that each task needs to be practised many times under the guidance of an adult before they are allowed or expected to be done alone. Tasks such as the visit to the local town need to be graduated. The journey needs to be done with an adult several times, encouraging them to take over each aspect of the journey in the adult's presence. Thinking through options for what to do when you are fearful, or when something goes wrong are always necessary even if met with a 'Yeah, yeah, yeah', or rolled eyes from the teenager. This does not mean you do not need to do it even for your own peace of mind! Teenagers can often listen well and respect your care, while looking as though they are not listening, therefore maintaining their cool demeanour.

Saying no and not being rushed into giving permission is crucial. Teenagers can often pounce on parents with requests or demands to go somewhere or do something. When the parent is expected to make a here-and-now decision, they need not simply comply. Instead, they could say something like 'That's an interesting proposal. I'll need time to consider it.' If the teenager persists with pressure and anger the parent can say, 'I may not be able to respond in the way that you want me to'. All requests require the parent to consider the consequences. It is a perfect opportunity to model how to use the pause button, to stop and think.

Negotiating Computer Time

Parents *do* need to check what their teenagers are doing online. They may protest, but privacy is earned with age and experience. Discuss who they talk to and how they know them. All too often, we read of predators using the online social networks posing as teenagers. Discuss with teenagers what they must do if they are asked to do or say things that make them feel uncomfortable. Sadly, I have met several young girls who have taken naked or semi-naked photos of themselves to share with their 'boyfriend', only to find these have been given a very public viewing. Adolescents need to know that nothing shared online is private, not even webcam conversations! Facts about privacy are essential, but of course parents must know them too!

Boundaries should be set for the time a computer is used, the place it is used (not in a bedroom) and permissions of use. Negotiate tasks to be done, such as tidying a bedroom, in order to earn the privilege of computer use. The notion of give and take needs to be continually reinforced throughout adolescence. The effects of not holding this boundary can result in the teenager further developing their single-minded journey, reinforcing the idea that life is 'all about me'. Reminding them that they are part of a family keeps open the opportunity for them to return to the family at times of need.

Praising Safe Behaviour

Celebrating and praising teenagers for tasks completed within safe boundaries not only helps them to create a sense of achievement and self-worth, but also allows them to feel valued and trusted. Both parent and teenager can reflect upon, and enjoy achievements throughout the journey into adulthood. Constant boundary setting and negotiation can create a negative relationship between parent and teenager. Noticing and praising times when the teenager has acted safely and sensibly helps both parent and teenager to reflect upon the positive.

Young people who often move into dangerous activities require their parents to reclaim control, starting with the most dangerous behaviour first. Power struggles may be minimised if the parent can find ways of demonstrating *why* it is dangerous and *why* they are re-negotiating the boundaries. Using a character from television may help to illustrate consequences of not redressing the balance of power. The most important message a teenager needs to hear is that because they are loved, their parents do not want them to continue this behaviour. Parents who have set boundaries that do not keep a teenager safe, need to openly admit that they have made a mistake.

Children of all ages learn valuable lessons from parents being 'wrong' about something. Making mistakes is an inevitable part of learning. Giving a young person permission to get it wrong allows them to make mistakes too.

'Should I Still Give Him Cuddles?'

Young people still require physical contact from their parents, albeit in a grab-it-and-run sort of way. This should not of course stop parents from showing physical affection; stroking their arms, or hair as they pass by or offering a cuddle, even though it may be rejected. Parents need to remember it is not them personally who is being rejected, but what that physical contact represents to the teenager.

Case Study – George (aged 15)

George, a fifteen-year-old boy, was deemed to be out of control. He was hanging around street corners with a group of friends smoking drugs, drinking, fighting and setting fires on waste ground. Subsequently he had been arrested by police several times.

George's parents struggled to live together and would argue regularly which often resulted in episodes of domestic violence. Although his father had left the house, George continued to feel unsafe at home. Fearing something dangerous might happen at any time activated his fear response, resulting in him wanting to be out of the house. His feelings of fear for his own safety were mixed with rage for 'not being man enough' to protect his mother from his father's violence. George's feelings of rage were calmed by the use of illicit drugs as an attempt to self-soothe. Drugs and alcohol temporarily calmed his rage; however it did not prevent him from lashing out at the world by smashing telephone boxes and lighting fires.

In helping George to talk about his feelings rather than simply carrying on acting them out, we found a scene of domestic violence on a television soap opera that mirrored his experiences. This helped him to name and understand his overwhelming feelings. Once George identified his fear, he was able to share extracts of the soap opera to his parents, helping them to identify how their behaviours affected him.

In Summary

The journey into adolescence is a struggle for both parents and the teenager. Parents need to be available, human, respectful and honest. They need to model negotiation, taking time to reflect, listen and empathise whilst providing very clear boundaries.

Teenagers need to be supported and trusted throughout the journey into adulthood. Both parties *will* get things wrong as well as right. Use of humour and the ability to reflect is essential for parents because it acts as a model of *how to be*. Remember, adolescence does not last forever and if parents and teenagers work together they are far more likely to prevent dangerous mistakes.

Bibliography

Batmanghelidjh C. (2006) *Shattered lives: Children who live with courage and dignity*, Jessica Kingsley Publishers, London.

Hughes D. (2006) *Building the Bonds of Attachment: Awakening Love in Deeply Troubled Children*, Rowman & Littlefield Publishers, Lanham, MD.

Morgan N. (2007) *Blame my brain: the amazing teenage brain revealed*, Walker Books, London.

Perry A. ed. (2009) *Teenagers and Attachment: Helping Adolescents Engage with Life and Learning*, Worth Publishing, London.

Sunderland M. (2007) *What every parent needs to know*, Dorling Kindersley, London.

Sunderland M. (2008) *Smasher*, Hinton House Publishers, Buckingham.

Wolf T. & Franks S. (2008) *Get out of my life … but first take me and Alex into town*, Profile Books, London.

Effective Interventions & Ways of Being with Angry, Traumatised Teenagers

Tracy Godfroy

This chapter looks at why teenagers can become so angry and alienated and how they can be helped to process, think about and *feel* their feelings rather than unconsciously acting them out or defending against them in detrimental ways.

Children who have experienced abuse, neglect and trauma in their early years often experience difficulties in maintaining relationships with others and are frequently seen to engage in chaotic, disturbed or anti-social behaviour. In the presence of stressful environments, the child unconsciously acts out or defends against their fears and anxieties. It does not occur to them to go to adults for solace and comfort. A child's behaviour becomes their language of communication (Vaughan 2005). Children who react with angry and aggressive behaviour to situational stressors tend to isolate and alienate themselves further when it is at exactly this time that they are in need of adult soothing and intervention.

In infants there are natural impulses and tendencies for healthy emotional development (Winnicott 1965; Schore 1999). Parents and other key adults are an essential part of this developmental process. In a physically safe environment an infant's cerebral activities will focus on learning and responding to the social and emotional signals of their parent-figure. (Schore 2003a, b; Siegel 1999). In contrast, where children have experiences of abuse, neglect or severe trauma, they lack the healthy kind of interpersonal experiences that are vital for the growth of the self. As a result, emotional development can be arrested. As the child grows up, they can be observed struggling to regulate intense feelings in socially acceptable ways. So, for example, they may be eight years old but their impulsive emotionally volatile behaviour is arrested at the age of a frequently tempestuous two-year-old. They can become angry, alienated and withdrawn from their parents, peers and other key people in their world.

A Framework Outlining the Stages of Psychological Growth in Angry Teenagers

Young people commonly present with challenging emotional and behavioural difficulties as a direct result of their experiences of abuse, trauma and neglect. It is helpful to look at the psychological growth of disturbed teenagers and the interventions they need in terms of three stages:

1   Calming the chaos – holding, containing and 'surviving'.

2   Reflecting on the feelings the teenager evokes in you and on their negative feelings towards you.

3   Forming attachments – psychological repair, consolidation and growth.

Stage 1: Calming the chaos – holding, containing and 'surviving'

The psychological disturbance in a child who displays chaotic, disturbed behaviour could be compared to the anguished cries of the infant who screams out panic and desperation. This child is in need of an immediate *containing* or *holding* response (Winnicott 1965) to help them find calm and peace again.

Four key relational interventions described by Kohut (1971) and Stern (1985) and many others can be summarised as:

✴ Empathic attunement (expressing deep understanding).

✴ Validation of the young person's subjective experience (acknowledging their feelings).

✴ Containment of feelings (being psychologically strong enough to stay emotionally regulated with the teenager – empathic and reflective).

✴ Soothing (tension regulation).

Without these forms of emotional responsiveness, the child will lack the emotional support needed to thrive. In the barren, desolate world of neglect or abuse a child may never have experienced what most take for granted in terms of love, care and emotional nurture. In this case, there is a significant risk of the child forming rigid, defensive and potentially self-destructive coping strategies. For many angry teenagers, the following is true: 'Since the joy of loving seems hopelessly barred to him, he may as well deliver himself over to the joy of hating and obtain what satisfaction he can out of that' (Fairbairn 1940).

Effective therapeutic conversation can, in some ways, repair and compensate for this developmental absence providing the listening adults can 'survive', feel and reflect on the intense feelings that the teenager is experiencing. The following case studies show the importance of the adult being able to contain their own intense feelings and help the teenager begin to regulate their feelings of inner distress.

Case Study – Katya (age 11)

Katya was not experiencing a good morning after receiving a call from her social worker informing her that a forthcoming contact visit with her father was to be postponed. Katya, I later found out, had destroyed her room, sworn at staff and cut holes in her trousers. She arrived to see me with a pen in hand, sat down on a beanbag and angrily drew in pen over her shredded trousers. I was quiet for a moment as I watched Katya discharge intense emotion into the scribbling action on the fabric. I quietly stood up and placed a large sheet of paper on the table in front of us. Katya hardly seemed to notice. I said, '*If you weren't allowed to scribble on your trousers, but could only use this piece of paper, what would that scribble look like?*'

Katya responded by drawing vigorously on the piece of paper in silence for some time before she began to draw less frantically and started to talk to me about her image. She said that her image was of a 'scribbly mess' (that she identified as herself and 'her family') in the middle of a maze, with no way out. Katya and I then began to make sense of her difficult morning in relation to the image and her underlying sense of despair in relation to familiar feelings of abandonment and rejection by her birth family.

Prior to this time we had together, Katya had been unable to think about seeking someone to help her to calm and soothe her intense feelings. Panksepp (1998) describes how intense emotions can rouse the mammalian brain into a 'fiery mental storm'. This gives an image of powerful emotional energies that need to be discharged. If this does not occur through steadfast and secure containment then they are likely to be discharged on to something or someone. Panksepp (1998) also describes anger as 'a special kind of internal pressure or force controlling one's actions and views of the world … that rapidly persuades us that the offending agent is below contempt and deserves harm'.

In Katya's case, the offending agent was her social worker, the building, and her care workers as she struggled to regulate her feelings and internal storms in socially acceptable ways. She eventually found a release through creating an art image with me: someone she felt psychologically safe with, because I was able to contain, empathise and soothe rather then criticise, shout and view her with contempt like so many adults in her life.

If an adult is to successfully 'contain' the teenager's 'fiery mental storms' they must remain psychologically strong enough, kind enough and calm enough to stay with the young person's intensely powerful feelings without collapsing, deflecting or retaliating. The adult's psychological stability regulates the teenager's intense emotional states, so that rather than moving into discharge or defence, the teenager will learn that it is possible to tolerate them, channel them creatively, and put them into words.

In my early experiences of therapeutic conversational work with disturbed children I learned a valuable lesson in how the process of maintaining physical boundaries can provide, on a parallel level, the psychological need for containment.

Case Study – Harinda (age 11)

Harinda had experienced sexual and physical inter-familial abuse from family members from birth until she was ten years old. She was removed from the family home and placed in foster care, where her high-risk behaviour (including approaching strangers, running away and mistreating animals) rapidly escalated and her placement quickly broke down. She arrived at the therapeutic community displaying signs of severe anxiety and distress.

In my time with Harinda I elected to make available some finger paints and a large piece of paper. She eagerly began to paint an image to reflect her feelings. I was keen to provide a space and material for Harinda to freely associate with, explore and represent what was uppermost in her mind. The session, however, quickly deteriorated as Harinda unconsciously demonstrated her lack of boundaries and containment by smearing paint first over the paper and then the table. I gently intervened, avoiding words such as 'no', or 'stop' but Harinda's levels of anxiety rose to the point of frenzy. Paint ended up over her apron, the table, the floor. Filled with anxiety, she ran from the room leaving a trail of dripping paint on door handles.

In subsequent sessions I addressed this incident with Harinda and while we later reflected positively on the incident as a benchmark of Harinda's psychological growth and development, it left me with a clear understanding of the importance of containment for intense feelings and anxieties. I learned that it is alright, in fact vital, to say 'no' to a teenager so as to define a boundary, and in future I decanted smaller amounts of paint until it was clear that the levels of chaotic behaviour had reduced!

The following case study is another example of the need for containment. The teenager began to act out while coming into contact with rising feelings of anger and rage.

Case Study – Siobhan (age 15)

Siobhan regularly engaged in serious self-harming behaviours including cutting, overdosing and attempting to tie ligatures around her neck. She had a history of inter-familial sexual abuse, trauma and neglect throughout her childhood years. More recently she had been subject to child sexual exploitation in her local community.

Siobhan was initially reluctant to work with me, stating that she didn't need any help. We agreed to meet for a six-week assessment period to decide together whether spending time together could be of benefit in helping to reduce her high-risk behaviours that various professionals, including myself, were so concerned about.

In one session, Siobhan and I were discussing her complex relationship with her mother when she became angry and withdrew from the conversation, looked away from me and started to state that she was bored and wanted to leave the session. When I gently enquired about what was happening, Siobhan appeared to become stuck and said 'I want to leave, I don't want to be here, I don't need any help'. She then began to strike the wall above her head with her fist. She hit the wall gently at first, as if to test my response. Quickly she turned her body further away from me and began to hit the wall hard with her fist, I believed with an intention to hurt her hand if possible. She was breaking away from our connection and becoming more preoccupied with causing harm to herself.

I wondered how destructive Siobhan might become to herself, or to the room or perhaps towards me. We had a contract of work that included not causing harm to herself in the room and I instantly thought that I could remind her of this. I chose not to, however, since I felt that this would antagonise her further. However, I think this choice stemmed more from my anxiety at the situation than from her relational needs in the moment. I chose instead to react firmly but calmly and tried to get her to engage with her anger and frustration in a different way.

The conversation went something like this:

'Siobhan, don't hit your hand … I don't want you to hit your hand.'

'You can't stop me'. [She continues to hit her hand very hard against wall. I consider other interventions available to me but decide for the moment to continue with firm, calm guidance.]

'I'm not talking about stopping you, I'm saying I don't want you to hit your hand. I don't want you to hurt yourself.'

[She continues to hit her hand but the frequency and intensity has decreased slightly.]

'Siobhan, I don't need to witness your violence against yourself, I want you to tell me how much you are hurting inside; I want to understand.'

[Siobhan stops hitting her hand against wall and turns to look at me with intensity.]

'Like you care, you don't care about me, nobody cares about me … nobody has ever cared about me, it's all bullshit. If they had, they would have come and got me when I was three, when they knew about [the abuse] instead of leaving me there for so long.'

'Yes [I said forcefully], you're angry, you're angry that nobody big enough came and stopped you from being hurt when you were three years old. And that meant that you kept being hurt until you were eleven, in your home Siobhan, the very place that you were supposed to be safe and looked after.'

[Siobhan bursts into tears.]

'No wonder you are so very, very angry, Siobhan.'

This significant intervention was one of several key moments in our work together that helped Siobhan to develop a deep sense of connection and trust with me. She continued to work with me beyond the six-week assessment period and regularly attended sessions until she moved to a new placement.

These three examples highlight the importance of the adult's role in calming the chaos and anguish in the teenager's internal and external world. In the next stage the teenager is more able to talk about or reflect on their life experiences.

Stage 2: Working with the feelings

The delinquent or disturbed teenager is encouraged to develop a trusting therapeutic relationship with the helping adult. At this stage, validation of a teenager's experience becomes a core element of the therapeutic task. Bion (1962a, b), has suggested that the process of 'alpha-functioning' (containing, processing and understanding intense feelings) is often deficient where a teenager has moved into delinquency.

It is therefore a crucial role of the adults concerned to be able to contain, validate, regulate and soothe so that the teenager feels safe enough to reflect on their feelings rather than just discharge them. The following case studies show a variety of ways in which a teenager can be enabled to reflect on their rage or anger about their past experiences in a safe way.

Case Study – Joanne (age 15)

Joanne experienced sexual and physical abuse from her mother, father and some of her elder brothers between birth and three years of age. She was removed from the family home and lived in a variety of foster placements until she was adopted at the age of six. Aged twelve, her adoptive placement broke down and she lived in numerous children's homes before arriving at the therapeutic community. Joanne's behaviour was extreme, chaotic and rivalrous, often driven by intense underlying emotions such as fear, panic and anxiety.

Joanne displayed disorganised patterns of attachment. In sessions with me, she presented as needy, demanding, psychologically and sometimes physically invasive. She would regularly employ a variety of behaviours designed to stop her leaving a session, so she could stay with me for longer. I generally felt adequately skilled to contain her feelings of anxiety, aggression and rage but knew on another level that I was not meeting her underlying unmet emotional needs.

Winnicott (1988) highlights that good technique must be 'more than just a corrective experience'. Through reflection on my own feelings in response to Joanne I felt I was not able to give Joanne enough of myself so that she could leave the session without raised levels of anxiety and acting-out behaviour. After one particularly difficult period of acting out at the end of the session, I said, 'Joanne, it seems as if I could spend all day and all evening with you and this still wouldn't feel like enough for you'. When Joanne spontaneously broke into a smile, I realised that I had really connected with her. From this point on, I could support her in developing a language around her desperately unmet emotional need of 'never having had enough of a mother's love'.

Joanne spent many sessions doing drawings, images and sand plays of 'enough love' and 'not enough love'. Although I could never provide enough for Joanne as a corrective experience, I could reflect on her pain and reflect back her non-verbal communication as useful and accessible data. I was 'failing' Joanne with an inadequate provision of what she felt she needed from me and in doing so I began to represent the mother who had earlier 'failed' to provide enough for her in infancy. Joanne was able to verbally attack me about that earlier (and now present) failure, while I survived and withstood these raging attacks (Casement 1985).

Through setting myself up as a willing and available participant, Joanne was able to hate me for failures or traumas that had come up as an environmental factor in her early childhood (Winnicott 1965) and our working relationship had much greater depth.

On other occasions, in working with teenagers experiencing anger, alienation and low self-esteem, I have found it very effective to use metaphors and images as part of the healing process. The following case study illustrates how I remained focused on the teenager's art image rather than being drawn into directly addressing her wish to leave the room.

Case Study – Sofia (age 12)

Sofia came to see me one week telling me she didn't want to talk with me, didn't want to stay in the room and that, in fact, she might only stay for a matter of minutes.

This was a familiar pattern at the start of our sessions although I noticed that Sofia was particularly agitated that morning. She kicked gently at a bucket as if to emphasise her point of irritation and potential for destruction then she noticed that the bucket contained Play-Doh. She picked up and began to mould the Play-Doh.

I noticed what she was doing and let her be for a moment. I reminded myself that she hadn't yet left the room. 'Well Sofia, I really hear how hard it is for you to be with me today … and that it's too hard to talk today … and …I'm noticing that your hands might be doing some talking with the Play-Doh?' Sofia thought for a moment before understanding my meaning and she snorted a muffled laugh. 'Yeah right', she replied curtly.

I had a moment of self-doubt and wondered if I should continue with this line of gentle enquiry given her volatile presentation that morning. I continued by heightening her sensory engagement with the Play-Doh: 'Squidge, squidge, squeeeeze, squeeeeze', I said as an accompaniment to her hand movements. She seemed to allow a connection to become established between us for a moment, until she abruptly slammed the shape onto the arm of her chair in an angry and defiant manner. She picked up more Play-Doh.

I stayed with what was happening with the Play-Doh rather than commenting on her anger and agitation 'Bang, you've arrived, hello Play-Doh image … wow, Sofia, can you tell me a little bit about your Play-Doh image? I see it's arrived, bang, on the arm of your chair'. 'Yeah, sure,' she said in a voice thick with sarcasm, 'it's an image of me'. She then slammed down the other piece of Play-Doh that she had barely begun to mould. Sarcastically she told me that this piece was an image of her mother. I felt that she was clearly telling me that she wasn't engaged with the arts materials and she didn't want to talk about anything today. It felt as if she was daring me to give up on her session and her image and give her permission to leave early. I didn't and I remained focused on the Play-Doh shapes.

I began to wonder aloud about the shapes, pausing every so often to check and observe Sofia's non-verbal communications. I noticed she was beginning to make more frequent, fleeting eye contact with me. I continued since she seemed to be tolerating my curious wonderings. Gradually, she became thoughtful about the image that she was creating, her body language became less agitated (her leg stopped shaking) and she began to caress the Play-Doh rather than handle it roughly.

'Well, I notice that you are very purple today Sofia,' I said, addressing the shape on the arm of the chair. 'I wonder how you feel about the colour purple?

And Mum, you are very green today. And I notice that there is a gap between you and Mum. In fact, you are both close to the edge of the arm, Sofia and Mum. I wonder what it is like in the gap between you? I wonder if the gap is big or small?'

At this point, Sofia had moulded a heart shape out of a third piece of Play-Doh and she placed this between the images of herself and her mother. 'This is a love heart', she said before tearing the heart down the middle and saying, 'Actually, it's ripped, it's a broken love heart'. Sofia left the silence in the room as if for me to fill.

'There's a broken love heart in between you and your mum,' I said, waiting for Sofia to make a comment. But I hadn't said enough. She seemed to be wanting more. I was aware of the powerful nature of the image and wondered what this meant to her. I tried to encourage her to stay in contact with the image and said, 'The broken love heart seems to be a bit closer to you, in fact it's almost touching you.'

Sofia then twisted the broken love heart to touch the Play-Doh image of herself. She merged her image into that of the heart. She also merged the image of her mother so that all three became a merged and twisted mass. She caressed the new shape in her hands, moulding and twisting. As she did so I said, 'And now there's no gap between you and your mum and the broken love heart'. Sofia was quiet but looked up at me. 'And I wonder, is that anything like how you feel about your mum right now?' Sofia said that she didn't know if that's how her mum felt about her. But she said that it was exactly how she felt about her mum, like there was a broken love heart between them. Sofia and I went on to talk about her difficult relationship with her mother and how hard it was for her to make sense of being placed outside of the family home, especially when her younger brother was still able to reside with his mother.

Sofia continued to regularly see me for several months and after this pivotal session she seemed to understand that she could now use Play-Doh, other art materials, images and metaphors to express her feelings. This was very important for her as she was able to identify that she sometimes felt very depressed and unable to say why she felt this way. At such times she could quickly become confrontational. During my time with her I saw Sofia flourish and her ability to express her feelings improved and her anxious and agitated behaviours reduced.

Case Study – Lisa (age 12)

When I first started seeing Lisa, she was keen to explore arts materials and appeared to be making a connection with me. But in subsequent weeks, which coincided with her finally beginning to settle into the therapeutic community, our relationship seemed to deteriorate rapidly, at least on a superficial level. Lisa would often leave early, or find it really difficult to come to the session on time and remain in the room. When she was in the room she would often refuse to engage in any conversation or activity. She appeared silent, moody, withdrawn and withholding and very, very angry. In one particular session, Lisa came into the room reluctantly and sat on a beanbag with her back to me. When I tried to reach out to Lisa she told me to shut up. She asked me to be quiet, to not speak and finally she asked me not to even look at her. Lisa became very angry when I did choose to speak. I was quiet for periods of time and I tried a variety of different interventions at other times.

Towards the end of the session I risked making Lisa very angry by introducing details that I knew about her life and by talking about her early experiences of family life. I knew that Lisa had lived with a succession of stepmothers, at least two of whom had been physically and emotionally abusive towards her. I said, 'I'm wondering if *you've* been asked to be quiet in the past Lisa, to not speak, to keep out of the way, and how difficult that must have been for you in your own home'. Lisa said nothing in immediate response to my comment but after a time she picked up a seashell from the basket and, for the first time, initiated a discussion about living by the coast. She reminisced about positive memories of her father taking her on fishing trips with her brother to the beach, just the three of them, no step-families involved.

For Lisa, Joanne and Sofia, the therapeutic space and safe relationship provided them each with an opportunity to be really heard and understood without blame or judgement. Issues touching on anger, alienation and low self-esteem manifest through very different presentations of acting-out behaviour. I tried to engage therapeutically with each teenager, and understand and address their underlying distress. Successfully negotiating this second stage begins to lay foundations for the teenager to begin to talk about their feelings and move towards forming a good working attachment relationship with the therapist.

Stage 3: Forming attachments – promoting psychological repair, consolidation and growth

If healing is to take place, a disturbed teenager must, over time, attach to an empathic adult. Research informs us that the part of the brain that plays a major part in processing emotional information and regulating emotional arousal (the prefrontal cortex) retains plasticity in adolescence. In other words, it remains totally open to positive change.

Therapeutic conversations, over a period of time, with an empathic adult help traumatised teenagers find words for feelings which in turn releases stress-moderating brain chemicals such as dopamine, serotonin and oxytocin. Over time biochemical states become personality traits. In other words, an angry teenager who is soothed, understood, and listened to is able to become a calm thoughtful adult. This is true both on a psychological and biochemical level. These chemicals regulate urgent feelings of rage, panic and distress and, if permitted to cascade the brain, they can provide all manner of 'heavenly feeling' states (Pennebaker 1993).

Case Study – Nikola (age 14)

Nikola had spent the morning engaging in disruptive behaviour including climbing onto the roof of a two-story building, being verbally aggressive and abusive towards others, and attempting to cause criminal damage. While she had a long history of anti-social, deviant and criminal behaviours, Nikola had recently made great efforts to reduce this high-risk behaviour and she had been engaging positively with her programme. The adults who were helping her were perplexed as to the sudden re-occurrence of the high-risk behaviour.

Fresh from her disturbed morning, Nikola stormed angrily into my room and initially appeared rude and highly defensive. Tense, she sat on a beanbag, looking 'shut down'. She was non-communicative apart from a standard response of 'I don't care'. I sat close to Nikola and could hear that she was trembling with each breath as she held emotional pain tight in her body. She seemed to be in need of a hug, but when I asked her this she replied emphatically that she didn't need a hug from anyone, she could look after herself.

I gently used a variety of different techniques to connect and engage with Nikola but she remained highly defensive. Then, I invited Nikola to stand up for a moment and look back at the beanbag as if she was still sitting on it. Something in this intervention caught her interest. Perhaps the invitation made Nikola curious. She stood up. I returned to my position on the beanbag and put my arm around the shoulders of an imaginary Nikola. I asked the standing Nikola, 'How would it feel if I did this?'

Nikola broke down and sobbed at the visual image that I had created. I invited her to come and sit on the beanbag and really be held. She did so and sobbed in my arms for a long time. Through the tears she said 'I've never felt wanted … I'm scared of being good and belonging [here] in case it goes away again'. Nikola and her younger sister had been adopted at an early age. Her adoptive placement later broke down and although her adoptive parents continue to care for her younger sister, they no longer kept in touch with Nikola. She also had a long history of being bullied and socially excluded.

Nikola begun to make attachments in the community and with me but this growing sense of belonging was unchartered territory for her and one that evoked fear and discomfort. It was easier and more familiar for her to act out and defend against these primitive feelings and tell herself she didn't want or need to belong anywhere and that she was better off on her own. As Mitchell (1988) writes, 'For someone who has experienced repeated failure of meaningful connection … hope is a very dangerous feeling'. After a time I was (eventually) able to reach the true feelings behind Nikola's angry and defended position. I connected with her authentic self and worked with her vulnerabilities and underlying emotional pain (Winnicott 1988).

Nikola was now more able to tolerate and process her emotional pain without moving into anger or rage. For Nikola the agony of having to leave two 'family' homes could never be repaired, not by me and not even if her mother 'came back' for her. What started to be repaired, contained and processed, however, were the overwhelming feelings of despair, anguish and abandonment.

Nikola was able to really engage well with me after this very significant time together. She had previously been very guarded and defensive, sometimes argumentative and challenging if she feared being exposed in anyway. After the 'imaginary hug' session she became generally more open and accessible to sharing vulnerable aspects of herself. She said it was as if she now felt that I was 'on her side' and that I could be trusted to have her best interests at heart.

Conclusion

Delinquent behaviour can be seen as wanton destructiveness or as a cry for help, and a symptom of a fragmented psyche born from experiences of abuse and neglect. If it is viewed as the former, we will continue to fail teenagers on catastrophic levels for both self and society. (Punishment alone doesn't work: 87 percent of young offenders re-offend.) This discussion has offered examples of effective interventions that go some way towards promoting psychological growth in troubled teenagers. The case studies show that teenagers can be helped to process and think about their feelings rather than simply discharge them impulsively. Furthermore, the therapeutic use of the arts offer vital communication tools for teenagers through a rich world of image and metaphor.

Bibliography

Balint M. (1995) *The Basic Fault: Therapeutic Aspects of Regression*, Grove Press, New York, NY.

Berne E. (1961) *Transactional Analysis in Psychotherapy*, Grove Press, New York, NY.

Bion W.R. (1962a) 'A theory of thinking', *International Journal of Psychoanalysis*, Vol. 43: 306–10.

Bion W.R. (1962b) *Learning from Experience*, Heinemann, London.

Casement P.J. (1985) *Learning from the Patient*, Tavistock, London & New York.

Fairbairn W.R.D. (1940) 'Schizoid Factors in the Personality', *Psychoanalytic Studies of the Personality* (1952) Tavistock, London.

Fosha D. (2000) *The transforming power of affect*, Basic Books, New York.

Giovacchini P.L. (ed.) (1990) 'The Implications of Winnicott's Contributions', *Tactics and Techniques in Psychoanalytic Therapy*, Vol. 3, Jason Aronson Publishers Inc., Northvale, NJ & London.

Hinshelwood R.D. (1998) *Psychoanalytic Psychotherapy in Institutional Settings*, Pestalozzi J., Frisch S., Hinshelwood R.D. & Houzel D. (eds), Karnac Books, London.

Hughes D. (2004) 'An Attachment-based Treatment of Maltreated Children and Young People', *Attachment and Human Development*, Vol. 6: 263–278, New York, NY.

James A. (2002) 'Container-contained: Psychoanalytically Informed Work in a Social Services Unit for Disturbed Adolescent Boys', *Therapeutic Communities*, Vol. 23:3.

Kohut H. (1971) *The Analysis of the Self*, International Universities Press, New York, NY.

Klein M. (1930) 'The importance of symbol-formation in the development of the ego', *The Writings of Melanie Klein: Love, Guilt and Reparation*, Vol. 1, Hogarth: London.

Metzler D.M. (1967) *The Psychoanalytic Process*, Heinemann, London.

Mitchell S. (1988) *Relational Concepts in Psychoanalysis: An Integration*, Cambridge MA, and Harvard University Press, London.

Panksepp J. (1998) *Affective Neuroscience: The Foundations of Human and Animal Emotions*, Oxford University Press, New York, NY.

Pennebaker J.W. (1993) *Emotion, Disclosure and Health*, American Psychological Association.

Porges S.W. (1997) 'Emotion: an evolutionary by-product of the neural regulation of the autonomic nervous system', Carter C.S., Kirkpatrick B. & Lederhandler I. (eds), *The integrative neurobiology of affiliation*, Annals of the New York Academy of Sciences.

Rousillon R. (1998) 'The role of institutional settings in symbolization', Pestalozzi J., Frisch S., Hinshelwood R.D. & Houzel D. (eds), *Psychoanalytic Psychotherapy in Institutional Settings*, Karnac Books, London.

Schore A.N. (1999) *Affect Regulation and the Origin of the Self: The Neurobiology of Emotional Development*, Lawrence Erlbaum Associates, Hillsdale NJ, & Hove.

Schore A.N. (2003a) *Affect Dysregulation and Disorders of the Self*, WW Norton, New York, NY & London.

Schore A.N. (2003b) *Affect Regulation and Repair of the Self*, WW Norton, New York, NY & London.

Siegel D.J. (1999) *The Developing Mind*, Guilford Press, New York, NY.

Stern D.N. (1985) *The Interpersonal World of the Infant: A View from Psychoanalysis and Development Psychology*, Basic Books, New York, NY.

Vaughan P.J. (2005) *Working with the Mentally Disordered Offender in the Community (Therapy in Practice)*, Nelson Thornes, Cheltenham.

Winnicott D. (1965) *The Maturational Process and the Facilitating Environment*, Hogarth, London.

Winnicott D. (1988) *Babies and Their Mothers*, Free Associations Ltd, London.

Healing Troubled Teenagers Through Relational Play with Toddlers

Dom Guard

This chapter will look at how making a connection with teenagers relies as much upon an adult's acceptance of adolescence as a necessary transition and their adoption of a non-judgemental stance, as it does on what is said or done by them. It will also examine the benefits of working with teenagers in groups, considering specifically the Teens & Toddlers programme. Originally designed as a practical teen pregnancy prevention, the programme matches troubled teens with toddlers in a twenty-week nursery placement. Through first facilitating, and then trusting that an attachment will be made, the teen is offered the opportunity to grow and explore their potential alongside a toddler who will also be fully involved in this burgeoning relationship.

Empowering Adults to Have Greater Understanding of, and Respect for, the Teenage Years

> I see no hope for the future of our people if they are dependent on the frivolous youth of today, for certainly all youth are reckless beyond words … when I was young, we were taught to be discreet and respectful of elders, but the present youth are exceedingly wise [disrespectful] and impatient of restraint.
>
> *(Hesiod 8th Century BC)*

In the 10 May 201 edition of *Psychologies* a readers' poll found that there were three main obstacles to talking to today's teenagers: 62 percent of adults felt they were out of touch with teenage interests: 28 percent said it was because of social networking sites and 10 percent said it was because parents or teenagers were never at home.

It seems that the problem adults have in relating to teenagers has not changed significantly over time. There have always been historical, social or technological changes that have altered adults' perception of teenagers, but these changes have increased dramatically in the twentieth and twenty-first century. There is little doubt that recently technology has moved at a rate more suited to the risk-taking teenage brain (Powell 2006).

New technology, like adolescence, appears to be a significant challenge for the majority of adults. I recently heard one adult complaining about 'Face Book, email, Twitter, blogs and the like' then adding, 'Teenagers just don't communicate anymore!' Even bearing in mind the socio-economic and technological changes between each generation, it could be argued that it is easy for parents to blame teenagers for 'not communicating', instead of looking at their own part in the problem.

If the behaviour of teenagers (literally, 'growers up') has remained the same and adults have always faced difficulties in communicating with them, how can this cycle be broken? In answer to this I would argue that just as some people talk of the need to be familiar with their own inner child in order to play with a child, to communicate successfully with a teenager one needs to acknowledge one's own *inner* teenager.

To facilitate this process the adult could recall and re-attune to the vitality of adolescence. This does not mean that the adult needs to become an expert on the teenage interests of the day but rather to think back to what mattered to them in their own teenage years. They could think about their experience of music in adolescence, perhaps a favourite song. They could consider how perhaps a lack of guidance, or a thirst for knowledge about relationships often led to a love of lyrics. Adults should respect the music of this teenage generation and give it the importance that they gave to vital tunes in their own adolescence.

If adults cannot connect fully with adolescence as a concept, a reality and as a time of massive changes in brain and body, then a relationship cannot be forged and the opportunity for healing intervention with too many troubled teenagers will be lost.

In my work with teenagers I have identified four successful ways of communicating that I invariably pass on to parents, carers or fellow professionals.

1   Avoid lectures: if you are talking in a repetitive, aggressive or sarcastic way which would get you hauled before an industrial tribunal at work, try another approach.

2   If possible, have your conversation on a shared journey. For example, a discussion on a car journey is often preferable to one at the breakfast table.

3   Talk about a shared experience. If possible, make the shared experience one that focuses on a favourite topic of the teenager experience: relationships.

4   Fun and play are essential ingredients of any environment that will enable any effective intervention.

As many of these teenagers are trapped in a cycle of rage or hate it may appear very difficult to implement any of the above. Trust now becomes the essential tool for the adult as they engage with teens who do not trust.

Groupwork with Teenagers

For some teenagers the therapeutic group can be too close in their minds to a (failed) classroom or family experience. These teenagers may initially be incapable of feeling secure in, or participating in groupwork (evidence of a 'disorganised or insecure group attachment', Brisch 2009). So it may be far more beneficial to see these teenagers on a one-to-one basis. In this context they can discuss their negative feelings about family groups or groups in schools.

If the teenager can be adequately supported and is receptive to this support then groupwork can be extremely beneficial.

The 'Teens & Toddlers' Programme – an Example of Groupwork Intervention

One initiative designed to help troubled teenagers has grown from the vision of Laura Huxley who founded the charity COUI (Children Our Ultimate Investment) in 1977. 'Teens & Toddlers' is a practical pregnancy prevention programme for both males and females which aims to foster an awareness of parenting and conception. The programme now runs across Britain and involves a highly structured curriculum that covers child development, self-esteem, peer pressure, identity, parenting, relationships and communication skills.

Each group has an optimum number of six teens and is supported by two facilitators who can come from a variety of backgrounds and are not necessarily therapists. The teens are chosen by their schools and each is then personally contracted into the project. The toddlers on the programme are four- or five-year-olds and are therefore toddlers in the American sense. Each teenager is invited to befriend a young child in a nursery setting for twenty weekly sessions.

This structured programme is very different from the offer of six weekly or open-ended individual therapy sessions and is well suited to teenagers who are struggling with anger, alienation and low self-esteem. As Geddes (2006) says, 'A well structured task for teens can offer an essential emotional safety net'. Each Teens & Toddlers project is planned extremely carefully and new facilitators always work initially with an experienced senior facilitator. The extensive and intensive training holds that each teen and toddler is learning how to empathise and that each teen is 'not yet a flower, but in a way it *is* a flower, it is *becoming a flower*,' (Whitmore 2004).

A clear confidentiality clause is negotiated and shared between the group. Wherever possible, the programme allows the teens to be both appropriately autonomous within the nursery setting and to be fully involved in the group process during their twenty week journey.

If a teen becomes overly fearful of the group process they are likely to withdraw from the project, leaving the group initially weakened but ultimately strengthened as they come together as a more cohesive and fully committed group. The insecure teens who can't manage the group might be better served by one-to-one work. If on the other hand, they are allowed to stay in the group they often try to split it, leaving members either intensely involved with them (seeing them as good) or rejecting them (seeing them as bad) (Brisch 2009). It is regularly explained to each teenager that they have choices and that they are continually making a choice as to whether or not they attend the programme.

Head and heart

The Teens and Toddlers programme is designed to engage the teen's head and heart. In the programme each teenager is invited to play imaginatively with, and to be responsible for, a designated toddler. The teenager will also attend theory classes covering topics such as communication and listening skills, in-utero and child development, human potential, the importance of parenting and fathers, conscious contraception, anger management and the choice of peers and sexual partners. Each topic invites reflection upon personal experience and this helps to hold the interest of the group and contributes to the formation of a working alliance. In the theory sessions, the issues of sexual relationships, love and contraception are also considered, using the concepts of choice, peer pressure and the emotional and social consequences of teen pregnancies. These issues are explained clearly and discussed with the aim of empowering the teens rather than lecturing them.

The combination of theory about human relationships and playtime with toddlers could be seen to represent an ideal curriculum for a teenager fluctuating between the states of childhood and adulthood.

The written work produced by the teens as part of the programme is judged not in terms of grammar or spelling but rather on thoughtful reflection and emotional literacy. Crucially, the teen who has failed too often at school is therefore not shamed or restricted in any way by their literary or academic capabilities. This approach allows the teens to succeed and allows their self-esteem to grow. Moreover, the facilitators must, at all times, present themselves as consistent role models and balance a sense of responsibility with an acceptance of the importance of humour and fun.

Empathy is encouraged at all times. Particular structured exercises are used to support this. For example, a toddler's physical point of view is acknowledged using an exercise where the teens take it in turns to tower over another teen who is on their knees. They are then encouraged to engage the toddlers on their level and to thus avoid talking down to them. The facilitator can then praise and respect the teen for praising and respecting their toddler.

Engaging and negotiating with the teenagers

Teens will not engage unless the adults around them are fully engaged. On the Teens & Toddlers programme each adult facilitator is carefully inducted on a comprehensive training programme in order to ensure they are capable of a full and non-judgemental engagement with the teenagers and that they develop an understanding and respect for adolescence as a developmental stage.

During the projects there is little time to negotiate when a real and possibly conflictive situation within the nursery requires immediate action. So part of the contract with each young person is that they agree to give the facilitator 'permission to coach' or to intervene if a situation becomes too hard for them or the toddler. After all, as a child the troubled teenager may well have had either no direction, or direction that involved physical or strong verbal chastisement. This, of course, is unacceptable with the toddlers. The teenager learns to accept that coaching and 'time out' are sometimes needed and this is done without shame and with the minimum of words to avoid lecturing them.

The following case studies will focus on the work done by two teens in a nursery setting and in a group.

Case Study – Leon (aged 14)

Leon was the only boy in the group, after a second chose not to join at all. When I first met Leon, I was unsure if he would, or should, join the group, since he had just been excluded from school for punching a teacher. When I encouraged Leon to come to the first session, rather than to wander the street, I was unsure whether I was making the right choice. I was anxious not just because he would be the only boy in the group but also because I wondered whether he would be safe to enter the nursery at all. (It is important to note here that as part of the contract with each secondary school, it is agreed that exclusion from school will never preclude a teen from attending a session.)

Leon walked slowly to the first session ('just to see it') and was largely taciturn but very briefly came alive when discussing his passion for boxing. This did not lessen my anxiety. However, Leon appeared to listen very well and after a brief tour of the nursery when the ground rules were provided by the nursery Head he said that he thought the Teens & Toddlers project was 'rubbish like school … only a bit better' and then asked 'When are we going to start playing properly?' Leon was enthused by the sight of the nursery activities. The boys and girls in the nursery were equally enthused by the relative rarity of a teenage boy in their midst.

Sadly Leon was often excluded from school during the twenty-week project. But he did not miss a Teens and Toddlers session and only once was a little late.

As I got to know Leon, I established that his father was in prison and that he 'no longer missed him'. Leon had experienced difficulty with his hearing until he was seven years old. He hated his primary (and secondary) schools, as he said he only ever heard the teachers 'when they were screaming at him' or as Leon put it, 'asking to be hit'.

When Leon returned to the nursery his thirst for (or a previous lack of access to) play was immediately evident and he would begin painting or playing in the sand as if he was five years old. He would play alone and be slightly annoyed that his enthusiasm for play appeared to magnetise an instant crowd around him. When Leon was told he was 'playing perfectly' by one of the teachers his grin was wide and long. In the second week when Leon was allocated his toddler, he began to structure his play and with help began to engage the toddler in reciprocal play. Leon found Andy, his very energetic toddler, funny and they would laugh regularly together.

In the seventh week, Leon met me on the way to the nursery school. He looked down and found it hard to keep eye contact. We chatted about boxing, before he asked me to buy him a sandwich and said that he would pay me back later. I bought the sandwich and he did not need to be asked to finish it before we entered the session.

Back in the classroom, after that seventh session, the subject of corporal punishment was discussed. We had already covered the concept of 'role models' and how the teen's behaviour would affect that of the toddler, and this appeared to be accepted by the group. Each member of the group slowly revealed they had been smacked and some fierce debate ensued about whether I was suggesting their parents were bad. Careful consideration was given to the difference between criticising a person and criticising their *behaviour* and how we might learn positively or negatively from an adult's behaviour.

Leon approached me half way through the ninth session after he had been struggling with his toddler. Leon and Andy had been playing pirates and making a ship with wooden bricks. I took care to match Leon's intensity and immediacy (Hughes 2004) as we discussed the incident:

'He [Andy] chucked a brick at me. I don't know what I am doing.'

'What are you doing?' I said.

'I don't know', said Leon. 'He won't do what I say.'

'What did you want him to do?'

'I don't know. But I want to hit him.'

'Thank you so much for letting me know, Leon. That's right on the money.'

'I don't like him. I don't know what to do.'

'That's great, letting me know. Maybe we can think about this together?'

After a long pause, and while looking somewhat aggressively at Andy who was occasionally checking in on us, shame-faced across the nursery room Leon said, 'I know hitting him teaches him to hit. Is that right?'

'What do you reckon?' I asked.

'What should I say? Should I say that I don't like that, 'cos we're not hurting anyone, right?'

'That's brilliant. Why don't we try that? By the way, I think Andy knows you didn't like that.' Leon looked again at Andy's clear shame and no longer looked back with aggression.

'And if it doesn't work I'll be back,' he said.

'I'll be right here.'

Leon returned to the pirate ship and boarded. Leon and Andy looked unsure as they set off on a new voyage. Both were unsure about how to negotiate the calm of unexpected peace and repair. But the play continued. Both looked victorious, as if something magical was happening in their play.

Leon had been triggered by Andy's aggression and had become enraged; he had sought help and bought time from me, acting as a secure base. From a neurological perspective he had been able to engage his prefrontal cortex (Perry 2006). This is the higher-thinking, reflecting part of the brain. Leon had calmed down and avoided what was set to be his default parenting position of meeting violence with violence. This was an excellent move forwards for Leon and was certainly the first time he had been congratulated for not hitting someone. It cannot be underestimated how hard this had been for him: to choose to avoid a well-established behaviour pattern. Leon had reflected on the situation, thought about his options, seen the possible consequences and made the right choice.

I am often met with incredulity by parents, carers or teachers when I suggest congratulating an aggressive child for not hitting. They do not appreciate how difficult it is for teenagers to give up fixed behaviour patterns that have worked so well for them over time.

I forgot all about whether buying him a sandwich was breaking a boundary. And I did not much care that I remained unpaid for it.

Case Study – Shasa (aged 14)

Shasa was very different from Leon in that she turned her anxieties inward. She also said she knew all the theory that she was being offered on the course. She was highly controlling and only settled in the group when she was allowed to scribe the lessons. She had elaborate handwriting and revelled in using coloured felt tips to design the class work on the white board. She quickly learned the Teens & Toddlers programme's core conditions for a healthy interpersonal relationship: empathy, respect and genuineness. Shasa had worked very hard in pulling the group together to accept the (non-negotiable) ground rules of the group, which included full attendance, no smoking, no cussing, no violence and no cross-talking. Shasa tried very hard not to cross-talk; it was something she usually did until she was excluded and labelled insolent or overly controlling.

Shasa revealed little about her background but it emerged that she was from a large complex family and appeared to be fighting for recognition at every step. She was quick to deflect any difficult situation onto her 'bestie' (her best friend Chelsea, who also attended) if she ever thought she had got something wrong.

When Shasa had to go into a classroom to remind another teen to attend a session she had the wholly inappropriate presentation of an irascible head teacher. The response from the interrupted teacher was extremely short and sharp. Shasa had acted as a controlling parent. I put this in the terms of transactional analysis (Berne1961) because it is a theory I would return to later with Shasa. After the exchange with the teacher Shasa's vulnerability was revealed in a blush that her grin belied. Shasa attended every session. She was apparently an ideal pupil and was always immaculately dressed and on time. But her excellence in the structured aspects of the curriculum was in stark contrast to the way in which she struggled to engage her toddler in reciprocal play.

Shasa was the eldest child in her family and her difficulty seemed to be that she had become a parent at an early age, in order to look after her younger siblings and had presumably gained recognition for leaving her childhood behind as quickly as possible. So while Leon took to the nursery relatively easily Shasa would only have entered easily if she had been given the job of head teacher. When she did enter the nursery she stayed close to Chelsea and took refuge wherever possible in disdainful giggling that was meant to imply that the tasks were beneath her. Shasa was linked with a very quiet toddler called Shannon. Shasa played in a very directive style and enjoyed both the responsibility of playing with Shannon and organising games of playing 'house'. Shannon felt safe but there was little fun and nothing reciprocal in the games.

Chelsea was, perhaps unsurprisingly, quite compliant herself and deferred to her best friend's organisational ability. However, sadly Chelsea found the group dynamic extremely hard and seemed at first to significantly regress and then to withdraw within the noisy nursery. When she decided that she would not attend again after the sixth session I agreed with her that she was making the right decision and had taken what she needed from the programme at this time. Shasa was left alone, with her toddler Shannon. Shasa showed no visible sign of regret that Chelsea had left and it later transpired that they had fallen out about a boyfriend over whom they had fought physically.

In the eighth week, I was struggling to see what Shasa and Shannon might gain from Shasa solidly maintaining a controlling, parent-like stance for twenty weeks in the nursery. I hung onto the idea that Shasa's defences were very important to her and, to quote the Teens and Toddler's own excellent and comprehensive manual: 'the teen is unique, with her own creative potential … the teen ultimately has all the answers … the facilitator validates the teen's human integrity and perceives the teen as more than just a problem to be solved'. Throughout the sessions I recalled an exercise whereby the facilitator is encouraged to experience what happens when a teen is regarded as a potential rather than a problem (promoted by COUI). The teenager is empowered, rather than controlled (Whitmore 2007), to become familiar with the core conditions of empathy, respect (prizing another) and congruence (genuineness). That said, I could not see Shasa easily being able to translate the theory into practice.

In the eleventh week Shannon did not attend due to illness. Shasa initially appeared lost without Shannon before I suggested she play with another toddler for that session. Shasa was quickly joined by another toddler and she briefly checked with me before spending this session with a highly energetic girl called Paulette. Shasa's instructions were ignored by Paulette who had no intention of playing 'house'. Paulette said she was going to play football and demanded that Shasa follow.

Shasa did not follow and noticing me, perhaps watching too intently, said, 'She thinks she is the boss. She ain't the boss. I ain't playing no football.'

I replied, 'Wow she is bossy isn't she?'

At this point Paulette looked back through the window from the play area and pushed her nose indignantly against the window. She left the window steamed up and departed to play alone. Shasa sat down, alone and disconsolate.

As I sat beside Shasa she said, 'She tried to make me feel like a little kid'.

'Then what happened?' I said.

'Like a little kid, an angry little kid. I felt like a little kid and I ain't no little kid', she said.

'No you are not. Funny though … that you felt like one.'

This was the first time that Shasa had shown any vulnerability at all.

After a prolonged silence I talked to Shasa a little about transactional analysis (Freed 1971). I explained the idea that we all have an adult, parent and child part of ourselves. And if someone presents themselves as a (bossy) controlling parent they are very likely to promote the response of a rebellious child in another person. Whereas accessing the 'thinking adult', 'nurturing parent' or 'playful child' part of our self is likely to encourage those same parts of another person to emerge. I also suggested that it only takes one person to change a relationship. Shasa listened attentively. She did not look as though she already knew this but the theory appeared to make perfect sense to her, especially when I applied it to her transaction with her own teacher which I had witnessed. Although transactional analysis is not part of the Teens & Toddlers programme, I estimated that I had met her on her own terms and that Shasa just might experiment with her own inner, nurturing parent and playful child.

Up to this point Shasa had been very wary about self-disclosure. But as we continued to talk I asked where she had gone to nursery and she revealed that she was in that nursery right now. I paused to consider what may have been a regression, before she revealed that she was not *feeling* like she was in it, but was actually in her old nursery school. I shared how difficult it can be for anyone to return to their old school. Shasa spent the rest of the session quietly and was joined by other toddlers as she slowly painted a colourful self-portrait. Shasa did not particularly engage with any other toddler.

When Shannon returned in the next and ninth week and greeted Shasa with a hug, the teen somewhat unexpectedly asked what her toddler wanted to play. Shannon, predictably, said 'House'. Shasa began to play more reciprocally and with great encouragement was able to let the toddler experiment and make mistakes. Shasa had almost definitely never had this experience herself. Towards the end of the programme I noticed with pleasure that Shasa was playing football with Paulette and Shannon. I heard Shasa say (loudly enough so that I could hear) 'I don't want to be doing this, but I am anyway'!

Two weeks before the end of the programme Shasa became more engaged in the group, She observed that, 'Leon is not being himself in the group'.

'How so?' I asked.

'He ain't usually like this. He can be real nasty out of here.'

'Perhaps he is experimenting with another part of himself,' I suggested.

Leon smiled broadly and playfully and Shasa nodded knowingly.

During their time at the nursery, both Shasa and Leon had explored parts of themselves that had previously remained dormant. Shasa had experimented with a more playful part of herself that helped her lose a fear of failure that was expressed as an over-powering need to control. Perhaps Leon's school tutor best expressed the change in him when he described him as a 'good kid', when at the outset he had been described as a 'bundle of trouble'; it was as though both Leon and his tutor could now see his potential.

Teenagers are necessarily trying out new identities; that is their job. Leon and Shasa had respectively and successfully experimented with responsible and playful identities.

The end and the future

All teenagers who have completed the programme are awarded an Interpersonal Skills National Award. As the final session ended, with sadness, goodbyes were said to the toddlers and cards given to the nursery teachers. As there were two hours until the ceremony at the Town Hall I let the teens make their own way there. When I arrived with my co-facilitator, and without the teens, a senior member of the project confidently predicted that they would not come for their awards, since 'they never come unless you bring them'. This made perfect sense. Getting an award was too alien to them; they had been allowed to think of themselves as failures. As I watched participants from other projects step up and receive their awards I contemplated what I had gently repeated to the teens over the last twenty weeks: that the ability to accept that a mistake has been made is crucial to growth.

As the ceremony drew to a close my teens burst in through the back door. They entered looking flustered and confused, but they were there. I introduced them and they received their awards. After the ceremony, Shasa explained that they had difficulty in getting in because they had arrived a little late. But, she added, 'I used some interpersonal whatsit and eventually they let us in.' 'That's brilliant, you are all brilliant,' I said.

I looked at them all and felt a deep sense of pride that I am sure they too were experiencing, both individually and together. I was left feeling that the growth of each individual within this group environment was crucial and that this had enabled them to accept and share their success. The focus of attention was dissipated by the group so that each individual could feel proud of themselves. As I watched them go, Leon turned back shyly and pushed the money for the sandwich into my hand. I accepted it warmly as I had grown to accept him: as a potential and not a problem.

A central tenant of the Teens & Toddlers programme is that (and according to Erik Erickson's eight stages of man) the toddler is essentially learning whether the world is trustworthy. Given that a troubled teen has not yet learnt to trust the world the essential stance of the facilitator is to trust and be trustworthy in this time of transition. The facilitator must hold in mind the teenager's unique personality and the fact that they are a vital and precious person with enormous potential. It is the belief and trust in the teens' potential which allows growth.

Research shows that 80 percent of teenagers ride the storm of their teenage years – relatively – successfully (Steinberg 1999). We need to support the other 20 percent. The Teens and Toddler programme is an excellent example of one way of providing effective support.

Bibliography

Berne E. (1961) *Transactional Analysis in Psychotherapy*, Grove Press Inc., New York, NY.
Brisch K.H. (2009) *Teenagers and Attachment*, Worth Publishing, London
Crittenden P. (2002) 'Transformations in Attachment Relationships in Adolescence: Adaptation Versus Need for Psychotherapy', online, www.patcrittenden.com

(Published in Spanish as: Transformaciones en las relaciones de apego en la adolescecia: Adaptación frente a necrsidad de psicoterapia. Revista de Psicoterpia, 12: 33–62.)

Erikson E. (1950) *Childhood and Society*, WW Norton and Company, New York, NY.

Freed A. (1971) *TA for Kids*, Jalmar Press, Sacramento, CA.

Geddes H. (2006) *Attachment in the Classroom*, Worth Publishing, London.

Hughes D. (2004) *Facilitating Developmental Attachment*, Rowman & Littlefield, Lanham, MD.

Perry B. (2006) *The Boy Who Was Raised as a Dog*, Basic Books, New York, NY.

Powell K. (2006) 'How does the Teenage Brain Work?' *Nature*, Vol.442, August.

Steinberg L. (1999) *Adolescence*, 5th edn, McGraw-Hill, New York, NY.

Whitmore D. (2004) *Psychosynthesis Counselling in Action*, Sage Publications, London.

Whitmore D. (2007) 'Working with at Risk Young People', online, www.teensandtoddlers.org/pdfs/ARTICLE%20Youth%20Development.pdf

This chapter is my independent and personal recollection of a Teens & Toddlers project. Further information, and evidence of the effect of Teens & Toddlers programmes, can be gained at www.teensandtoddlers.org

Body-Based Interventions for Troubled Teenagers

Louis Sydney

> 'Traumatic events are extraordinary, not because they occur rarely, but rather because they overwhelm the ordinary human adaptations to life … the common denominator is a feeling of intense fear, helplessness, loss of control and threat of annihilation'.
>
> *(Herman 1992)*

This chapter focuses on body-based (somatic) interventions with teenagers who have suffered trauma. Two case studies illustrate two of the central presenting styles most often seen in teenagers who have experienced trauma, namely emotional numbing and the opposite, hyper-arousal. The physiological issues relating to these states are discussed and effective interventions offered.

There is a growing awareness of the benefits of using body-based interventions with young people who have been traumatised. Trauma response teams, such as those who respond to suicide bombing disasters, are likely to have some understanding of, or skills in, helping people whose bodies and physiological condition are in a state of being overwhelmed. These distressing states may be experienced by people as panic attacks, nightmares or sleep disorders, flashbacks (to the terrifying event), hyper-vigilance and physical complaints such as stomach and chest pains that seem hard to alleviate with any medication.

A specialist trauma response team, trained in Peter Levine's body-orientated therapy (described in his book, *Waking the Tiger*,1997), provided community focused interventions after the tsunami disaster in Thailand in order to address the internalised terror, fear and anxiety the disaster had engendered. Many of the community displayed extremely heightened levels of stress, their bodies still vigilant and in readiness for more physical threat.

The human brain responds to perceived threat in a primitive way, by moving into fight, flight or freeze reactions. If this survival and defence system is not successful or effective in its efforts to mobilise the body towards safety, then it is possible that stress levels overwhelm the physiological system and leave a residue of physical (somatic), emotional and cognitive impairment that can dramatically affect a person's ability to function in the world.

Case Study

A 16-year-old girl who had been a passenger in a bad car crash was suffering from Post Traumatic Stress Disorder. She found it extremely difficult to be in a car again after the accident and was experiencing heightened anxiety before travel. She also had nightmares. When she did travel in a car, it was common for her to find herself 'bracing' as the car accelerated or braked.

These are not unusual symptoms for people who have experienced some form of car accident, as the human brain tends to react to a perceived overwhelming threat with involuntary responses. The human brain, sometimes referred to as the triune brain (a concept originated by Paul MacLean) can be roughly divided into three areas: the reptilian brain (instinctual), the mammalian or limbic brain (emotional) and the frontal lobes (reflective and rational). The physical sensation of a car braking can trigger the more primitive reptilian area of the brain in a person who has suffered a car crash. As a result, the car braking can be experienced as potentially life threatening. It is in such situations that human beings are physiologically mobilised to move into a fight, flight or immobilised response, i.e., they attempt to flee a dangerous situation (flight), confront a situation (fight) or become overwhelmed by their terror and do nothing (freeze).

When Traumatised Teenagers are Referred for Help

Traumatised teenagers can present in two very different ways:

✹ 'Angry', oppositional, explosive, *hyperactive*, 'acts out' in terms of anti-social behaviour.

✹ Withdrawn, overly compliant, *low key*, switched off, emotionally numb, who internalises (attacks self rather than others, e.g., self-harm, puts self down). With both of these groups, awareness of body and physical behaviour can provide some insight into what interventions may be required in the future. Levine (1997) makes clear that 'the key to healing traumatic symptoms is in our physiology'.

Working with Angry, Explosive, Hyperactive Teenagers

The referral of an angry, agitated, 'acting out' teenager is far more common than the switched off, withdrawn and 'acting in' type of teenager. This is because these young people are inevitably far more disruptive to their families, schools and the environment. Increasing financial resources are used to contain, control and ultimately change or modify the behaviour of increasing numbers of teenagers, often with very little success because the underlying trauma has not been addressed. The high rate of re-offending among young offenders is indicative of this. If we are to work effectively with the trauma, bodily hyper-arousal must be addressed. The aim of the therapeutic work is to reduce the repeated state of high arousal by identifying triggers, developing awareness of bodily responses and enabling self-soothing.

Case Study – Kevin (age 15)

Kevin had been living in foster care for five months after assaulting his adoptive mother. The physical attack had involved him threatening her with a knife and finally punching her in the face. Kevin was adopted at five years old and had always struggled to manage his aggression. His early life history had involved being physically and emotionally abused and he had suffered extreme neglect.

The aim of my therapeutic work was to assess what level of contact Kevin might have with his adoptive parents and to explore to what extent he still represented a risk to his parents. His foster carer advised me that he could be like a 'bear in a pit' if he was agitated. However, I was also asked to explore whether a body-mind approach to working with Kevin could help with his angry outbursts. Kevin's behaviour, in fact, presented as a biological re-enactment of his early life trauma. In some ways it could be considered as a survival strategy which had once served a purpose (survival) but now hindered Kevin's life. Trauma-related acting-out behaviour has been described as 'an unsuccessful attempt to discharge the intense energy mobilised at the time of the trauma, to defend against a perceived life threatening experience' (Levine 1997).

When I met Kevin, I shook his hand and could see that he was tense, physically tight and had a tendency to tap his feet in agitation when he sat down. Having confirmed that he understood why he was meeting me, I spent a few moments trying to create a relaxed environment and made comments about his 'hoodie' and asked about its design. This was a deliberate intervention that aimed to show to Kevin a genuine interest and curiosity about who he was and what mattered to him. I then acknowledged what I imagined he might have been feeling upon meeting me, saying: 'I guess Kevin that a part of you may be thinking, here's another assessment with some balding bloke trying to ask me questions again!' This style of trying to engage with Kevin, using some mild self-deprecation and showing empathy with his predicament of being assessed yet again is an approach used by clinical psychologist Dan Hughes. It is part of his attachment-focused therapeutic model PACE: Play, Acceptance, Curiosity and Empathy (2009). Kevin appeared to relax. His shoulders dropped and he smiled and made eye contact briefly.

Working with Trauma Through the Body

Stage One. Focusing on the immediate environment: orientation

I asked Kevin if he would take part in, '… a quick quiz I use with all young people to see how awake they are!' He smiled and shrugged again in a way that said, 'If you want'.

I then asked him a number of sensory-based (sight, smell, hearing and touch-related) questions:

✳ Can you point to three things in the room that are blue?

✳ Can you tell me how many shelves there are in that recess?

✳ Can you tell me three things in the room that you might like the feel of?

✳ Can you tell me three things you can hear apart from the sound of my voice?

✳ Can you point to three things in the room that are red or have red in them?

✳ Can you tell me three things in the room that are made of wood?

✳ How many eyeballs are there in the room?

These apparently trivial questions have a purpose. By inviting Kevin to answer such questions that make him focus on his immediate environment, his brain and mind have to *orientate* to the present and to his immediate surroundings. This approach can be helpful when working with young people who have experienced early life trauma and appear vigilant to their surroundings, fearful about what might happen, caught in a fight/flight response to the world. We know that focusing on the here-and-now environment using sensory involvement can help to alleviate this tension.

Stage Two. Building a relationship: establishing safety

The next few sessions were spent building our relationship and working alliance. At this stage, I was surprised and impressed by Kevin's efforts to engage in the process of thinking about his situation in foster care. I discovered that he was creative (even though he did not think he was artistic in any way) and he enjoyed music, films, graffiti and anime art. He also loved to watch documentaries about wild animals, relaying a variety of facts and figures about different animals of prey.

Milton Erikson (1980) emphasised the importance of helping people to resolve their problems by *utilising* whatever natural assets, interests or skills they possess. Kevin's interests in television soap operas and wild animals enabled me to make an attempt at 'meaning making' and normalisation of his particular interests. In other words, helping Kevin make connections as to *why* he had such interests. He could take on board the fact that his interest in wild animal documentaries was an expression of a part of *him* that sometimes felt like the predator and sometimes like the prey in the documentaries. I also spent time validating Kevin's experience and explaining that his symptoms were in fact normal physiological responses to an extraordinary situation (his early life trauma) and hence enabling a 're-framing' of his symptoms.

Many teenagers living with un-worked-through trauma have not been understood and are pathologised for their physiologically predictable responses to stress, which manifest in challenging behaviour. I explained to Kevin that his early life trauma and experience of neglect and domestic violence had wired his brain and body to be ready for these awful things to happen again at any time. Even though there was in fact no violence in his current life, his body was still primed and expecting 'bad stuff' to happen. I could see that Kevin was engaged with what I was saying, which is vital if a teenager is going to invest in the therapeutic process. When working with trauma and using a body-orientated approach, some basic explanation of what is happening physiologically can be helpful in order to help teenagers understand their experience more fully.

In the next session, I again engaged Kevin's personal interest by bringing in a DVD about wild animals. One scene showed a cheetah hunting an antelope until it caught and then devoured it. I asked Kevin to watch the scene once more imagining that he was the cheetah. I then asked him to 'sense' any feelings in his body and report to me what he felt. He described his heart beating fast, his legs feeling light and strong and a 'weird' sense that he could see really well. Once again, I showed him the film, this time asking him to imagine that he was the antelope. He anticipated my questions by beginning to tell me what he could sense in his body … a tightness in his chest, a fluttery tummy and, interestingly, a discomfort in his bowel area. (It is not uncommon for animals being hunted to urinate as they are fleeing as a way of emptying excess fluid and enhancing the ability to escape.) Many humans also feel the need to defecate when they are about to take part in something that makes them nervous, such as a sporting activity or public speaking.

Kevin was quite taken by the contrast of the two experiences and I suggested to him that when he was a young child suffering early life trauma, his body would have experienced a similar kind of terror to that of the antelope. Kevin immediately got the idea (and a quickly drawn diagram helped) that the alarm systems in his brain and body were still highly activated and that he had not learned to switch off and nor had his brain learned that he was now safe.

Stage Three. Awareness of physiological body states: self-monitoring and recognising triggers

My therapeutic work with Kevin became characterised by routine check-ins and check-outs at the beginning and end of sessions to help Kevin to observe his physiological body states, that is, what he was feeling in his body, any sensations or tensions. Ogden (2006) states that 'through the mindfulness of present moment organisations of experience, [the person] shifts from being caught up in the story and upset about her reactions to becoming curious about them'. This gentle process of self-observation enabled Kevin to become more curious and explore his experience. Increasingly, Kevin became aware of the triggers and situations that would normally distress him. I encouraged him to imagine challenging scenarios in his day-to-day life, while sensing his bodily responses. Over time, this *dual processing* allowed Kevin to develop a greater ability to tolerate perceived stress and anxiety and move closer towards a position of calm reflection.

This work with Kevin involved several vital areas of intervention for treating traumatised teenagers, including using Dan Hughes' PACE model as a way of developing a rapport and establishing an engaging, warm, empathic and curious approach to relationships.

✳ Utilising the teenager's current interests as a tool for intervention.

✳ Developing the teenager's capacity to self-monitor and become aware of their own body states and internal states of arousal.

✳ Using these skills to better understand the physiological cues and signals that can indicate to the teenager that they might be about to blow.

✳ Helping the teenager to become more aware of how and what in the immediate environment may trigger a response of fight, flight or freeze.

✳ Providing the teenager with some basic information (psycho-education) that explains what is happening to them physiologically and how this is a *normal* body-mind response to (what they perceive as) a frightening situation.

✳ Learning to negotiate, practise and rehearse better responses to relational stress in order to gain a greater sense of personal mastery and self-esteem.

Slowly, Kevin was able to allow himself to express and feel the previously feared feelings of anxiety, rage and abandonment regarding his early life trauma. This lessened his need for primitive fight responses to the stressful situations he encountered a survival strategy and way of communicating his feelings.

Working with Withdrawn, Emotionally Cut Off Teenagers

The referral of a switched-off, shy, withdrawn and 'acting in' teenager, can be immensely challenging. Often, these young people have been 'beneath the radar' of therapeutic services and help in primary schools, because they may have been considered cute, charming, compliant and 'no trouble'. As a result, their symptoms have become more entrenched by the time they reach adolescence. It is not uncommon for these young people to seek drugs, alcohol or self-harm as a way of self-stimulation or muting internal anxiety and stress. For teenagers who present as emotionally cut off, there is a fundamental disconnection between the teenager and their experience, their feelings and their body. It is as if their spirit has died. It is vital to keep in mind that withdrawn, shut off 'defences' have been adapted as a much needed survival strategy for what was experienced as overwhelming or terrifying. Therefore, it can be helpful to remember that beneath the calm or withdrawn exterior is a highly fearful and anxious person who has a significant investment in maintaining control and thus perceived safety and who is resistant to change.

When using a body-focused approach with a teenager who may have a physical 'low tone' (slouched or floppy) and is seemingly compliant and withdrawn, the aim of the work is to:

✳ Develop awareness of bodily responses.

✳ Increase awareness of sensations in terms of perceived triggers or stressors.

✳ Increase the ability to externalise feelings and thoughts of emotional experiences through the use of arts-based work.

✳ Enable self-soothing.

Case Study – Anna (age 13)

Anna's mother had been diagnosed with mental health issues. Anna was the oldest of three siblings and in many ways was a 'parentified' child, in the sense that she had assumed the role of being a parent to her siblings and also her mother. Anna's mother had a history of being unpredictable and physically threatening. She would leave the home without prior warning and when at home could often be physically and emotionally needy, particularly after consuming excess alcohol.

When I met Anna, her quiet, compliant manner was very worrying and she appeared to 'drift off' and dissociate if I spoke for too long. After bringing her attention back from her dissociative state, she could not remember what I had been saying. Dissociation has been described as a kind of 'spaciness', a breakdown in the continuity of a person's 'going on being' which 'almost always includes distortions of time and perception' (Levine 1997). Dissociation is a common body-mind response to trauma when the person has experienced overwhelming fear. It can lead to chronic problems in terms of thought disorders, problems with attention and concentration, body-based problems and emotional problems. In contrast to Kevin, whose physiological response to stress was *vigilance*, Anna's response was *avoidance* and *cutting off*. Anna also took little care of herself physically, and her personal hygiene was poor, which reflected her neglectful environment at home.

Using sensory exercises to enable sensitisation

As in Kevin's case, I used sensory exercises at the beginning of our times together to help Anna shift to a less avoidant position and to enable her to become more sensitised to her environment. I also introduced the idea of some basic yoga or stretching at the beginning and end of our sessions, as a way of 'warming up' and 'winding up' our work together. This was a deliberate intervention to work with her marked slouch and collapsed physical presentation, both of which are indicative of a body that has been overwhelmed. This process was difficult at first as Anna reacted with a 'can't do this' approach as I challenged her to move out of her comfort zone.

I again used Dan Hughes' approach of being somewhat playful and engaged which seemed to enable and evoke Anna's personal interest in the process.

I also introduced on-going body sensing and self-reporting. The aim of this approach was to enable Anna to begin a process of becoming more sensitised to her immediate environment. Frank (2001) describes the necessity of helping people 'to organise their awareness so that they experience themselves as part of, rather than alienated from their environment'. She goes on to say that 'one of the most important initial therapeutic interventions is to ask the person *how* they sense themselves sitting on the chair or how they sense the floor beneath their feet'. This is known as the process of *orientation*. In Anna's case, it simply involved asking her to slowly notice, sense and describe her body (inside and out) from her head down to her toes. This included asking her to sense what her tongue felt like, her lungs and breathing, the joints in her arms and legs and even noticing her back, buttocks and feet and where they came into contact with the chair or the floor. I finally asked her where in her body she felt comfortable or uncomfortable. The therapeutic aims included enabling Anna to:

✳ Develop a greater capacity for identifying and tolerating her anxiety states.

✳ Learn that by the practice of noticing her body from head to toe, she would be more able to regulate (soothe or calm) herself.

✳ Learn to 'associate', that is, to be present in the moment rather than to dissociate (to cut off from the present moment).

✳ Develop a more mindful approach with a greater awareness of 'here and now' rather than keep getting pulled back to her traumatic past – the 'there and then'.

Using art and creativity

I quickly realised that talking and a more cognitive approach did not fully engage Anna as she often seemed to switch off. So, I introduced arts-based, creative ways of working and made sure that when I did speak, I used shorter and more concise sentences to hold her attention. This approach seemed to facilitate the therapeutic work and it complemented Anna's need to be one step removed from her troubled life. Using arts, clay and play allowed Anna to gain safe psychological distance from what was emotionally charged material. It also enabled her to communicate to me about her inner world and express herself in ways that were simply not possible when working only verbally. Anna was much more able to draw or paint her story of life at home and also make images of the feelings in her body.

Increasingly, I began to realise that I could utilise Anna's interests in pop music, writing poems and stories. The themes and images of her stories involved over-bearing witches, abandoned children who were eaten alive by monsters and dark scary houses. Anna was delighted to write an 'imaginary' fairy story about her life, and its graphic imagery enabled her to explore her traumatic home life. After a while, with Anna enacting stories through drama, and playing the various roles of devoured children, insatiable monsters, wicked witches, there was a very hopeful shift in her play. A benevolent wizard appeared. The emergence of this benign and potent positive figure within her narrative was a healthy development . The wise wizard was able to forgive and accept the 'evil behaviour' of the others. This reflected a period in our time together when Anna became more able to accept herself and most importantly, to no longer blame herself for her parent's inability to care for her appropriately.

When seen as a whole, the role plays represented a shift from her previously disembodied way of being in the world, to a far more 'embodied' sense of self. Anna was clearly doing more than acting a role in a story. Her physical, dramatised and verbal expression of stories, illustrating the themes of her difficult life, allowed her to make far more sense of her very troubled early life experiences. This 'kinaesthetic' (Haen 2008) reclaiming of the body also enabled Anna to 'rehearse the possible' within her dramas and through her imagination. She introduced powerful animal spirit characters that were able to transform and enchant the future. At various points in her portrayal of these characters, I asked Anna to pause, and to sense and describe how she felt in her body. She described a sensation of rising energy through her legs and chest and a tingling in her fingers, and she was amused and elated when I described how tall she looked and how twinkly her eyes appeared. I also took time at the end of the role-plays to 'stretch down' as an attempt to integrate her experience and ensure that she took time to notice her breathing and to relax. It is often the case that by simply noticing one's breath and maintaining one's attention that breathing begins to regulate itself. This was certainly the case for Anna who became fascinated by her regular tendency to sigh deeply when observing her breathing for the first time. For Anna, it was a sign that 'I had kind of forgotten myself, and by breathing … now I've come back to myself!'

At the end of our time together, Anna presented as a far more grounded teenager who was more able to express her needs and choices. She had also entered a phase of being less compliant at home and instead she'd become more resistant, which one could speculate was a relatively healthy response and shift from the 'parent-like' child she had always been. In the past, Anna had prioritised the needs of her emotionally fragile mother over her own, which had led to her always minimising her own feelings. This positive change created a further issue in terms of my helping Anna to have her needs met and ensuring that her mother received on-going support to be able to parent Anna in a different, healthier way. Anna was also referred to a local Mentor in the community who was able to meet her regularly and offer additional support.

Following periodic review meetings with Anna to gauge her progress, I noticed that she had begun to take more care of herself physically, she dressed better, began to exercise, her hygiene was good and she rarely drifted off in our meetings.

Somatic Psychology

Embracing body-orientated or somatic psychology as an aspect of how to work with troubled teenagers can be essential, particularly when addressing trauma. The practitioner does not need to be an expert in bodywork, as simply having a mindful awareness towards body sensations and responses can offer a rich source of opportunity for self-understanding and personal insight. Careful observation of skin tone, posture and physical energy states, combined with on-going enquiry that explores what the teenager feels or senses in their body can offer useful information.

Through on-going self-observation of physical responses it is also possible to develop greater potential for self-regulation (self-soothing) and co-regulation (allowing soothing from others). Siegel (2005) describes how the both the heart and stomach area (or the intestines) operate not only as organs of circulation but also of *perception*. It is common to hear people say they are 'speaking from the heart' or describing their 'gut feelings'. This integration of cognitive, physical and emotional aspects of experience can develop a more embodied and grounded 'felt sense of self'. The felt sense offers a deeper feeling of well-being, connection and vitality.

In young people, there are a multitude of physical changes occurring over which they have no control: hormones, body hair, acne, change of voice, sexual drives and more besides!

A mindful, curious and empathic approach to including the body in the process of healing may serve to deepen a teenager's ability to manage the transition into adulthood and offer a greater sense of control and autonomy.

Bibliography

Erikson M. (1980) 'Deep Hypnosis and its Induction', from the collected papers of Milton Erikson.

Frank R. (2001) *Body of Awareness: A somatic and developmental approach to Psychotherapy*, Gestalt Journal Press, Gouldsboro, ME.

Haen C. (2008) 'Vanquishing Monsters: Drama Therapy for Treating Childhood Trauma in the Group Setting', in Malchiodi C.A. (ed.), *Creative Interventions with Traumatised Children*, Guilford Publications, New York, NY.

Herman J. (1992) *Trauma and Recovery*, Pandora Books, London.

Hughes D. (2009) *Attachment Focussed Parenting*, WW Norton, New York, NY.

Levine P. (1997) *Waking the Tiger*, North Atlantic Books, Berkeley, CA.

Ogden P. (2006) *Trauma and the Body*, WW Norton & Company, New York, NY.

Siegel D. (2005) 'The Mindful Brain', Paper presented at the *Emotion Meets Spirit* conference, Watsonville, CA.

School-Based Anger Management Programmes & the Therapeutic Use of the Arts

Louise Bartel

This chapter explores why teenagers have such a reputation for angry outbursts and destructive behaviour. It considers the neurobiological reasons, the environmental factors and the comfort that anger can offer troubled adolescents as a defence mechanism. Drawing directly on my own experiences of working with young people, this chapter offers interventions for facilitating change, to enable adolescents to address their anger. These interventions include structured school-based anger management programmes, alongside therapeutic counselling using the arts. Both interventions aim to identify key strategies for releasing anger in a positive manner and educating teenagers about ways of calming themselves and reaching a state of emotional homeostasis.

The structured programme is largely educational, exploring teenagers' individual anger styles and possible origins of their anger. At the end of the programme teenagers produce their own anger management Personal Strategy Plan, which identifies key strategies that they have agreed to implement as a positive attempt to manage their anger in a safe and socially appropriate manner. The therapeutic use of the arts is also considered as an alternative way of helping troubled teenagers, offering them a safe outlet for feelings of anger, rage and distress. Three case studies demonstrating that the arts can provide a vehicle and container for expressing and exploring difficult or painful emotions are also discussed.

> Anger is healthy. Anger is passion, resilience, being alive, engaging … it fuels creativity. It gets things done.
>
> *(Luxmoore 2006)*

The crucial factor, however, is *how* anger is expressed. Barely a day passes without news reports about angry teenagers, gangs, violence and weapons. People are scared of these teenagers and '… everyone is crossing the road to avoid the "hoodie generation"' (Batmanghelidjh 2009). People feel powerless, at a loss as to what might effectively address this anger epidemic. Ironically, the angry teenagers themselves are often experiencing similar feelings; confusion, fear, frustration, the sense of being unimportant, and the feeling that their voice goes unheard. So how can they make people listen? By using the most powerful emotion they know: anger. Through anger they can vent anxiety, frustrations and their sense of injustice.

Anger as a Healthy Expression

Everybody experiences anger. However, being faced with an angry and aggressive person often triggers one of three instinctual responses: fight, flight or freeze. As a consequence people are aggressive back (either verbally or physically), or they retreat, or feel emotionally numb to the situation. Society often conveys the message that anger should not be expressed, that it has no social acceptability and those who do express it need help to 'get rid of it'. But anger is a fundamental human emotion and expressing it in a healthy way is important. Adolescents often need help to learn how to vent anger as a 'healthy expression'. Understanding anger and learning how to release the intense emotional charge in a safer manner, is at the core of the work with many teenagers referred for 'anger management' courses, either within or outside of the school environment.

Neuroscientific Reasons for Teenage Anger

Learning about the neurobiology of adolescence helps us to understand the tendency for many teenagers to respond to situations with anger. It is important to be aware that the frontal lobes are still developing throughout the teenage years (Giedd et al 1999). The frontal lobes are the part of the brain that enable reasoning and reflection, planning ahead, impulse control, organisational skills and stress regulation. With a limited ability to do these things teenagers are often caught in the instinctive response of 'fight, flight or freeze'. They tend to react first and think later.

James Crist (2008) uses the analogy of driving a car to explain what is happening in an adolescent's brain as it responds to threat. 'Imagine that your brain is a car. Normally your frontal lobes are in control. Now imagine you're driving down the road when you see something that triggers your anger. The old mammalian and reptilian parts of the brain reach over and grab the steering wheel and the next thing you know you're swerving out of control.'

Neurobiological changes in the teenage brain also impact on their ability to correctly identify emotion in others. This is a significant factor in determining how teenagers react to other people. In a Harvard study led by Deborah Yurgelun-Todd (2002) brain scans of adults and adolescents were taken while they were engaged in the task of naming emotions from pictures of facial expressions. The scans highlighted the differences in brain activity. The brain activity of the adult participants concentrated around the frontal lobes, while the activity in the adolescents was found to be focused in the limbic system and in particular the amygdala. As a consequence the adult participants demonstrated a much greater ability to name emotions correctly. The adolescents, on the other hand, often wrongly identified emotions; for example, they incorrectly saw fear as shock, surprise, and even anger. This begins to explain why adolescents frequently perceive anger and hostility in others when none is present and why they respond defensively.

The relevance of attachment to teenage anger

It is also vital to take into consideration the attachment relationship the teenager has with their parents. This is fundamental to their ability to remain psychologically strong in the face of adversity. A secure attachment is also key to the teenager's capacity to empathise, reflect and regulate stress. This attachment to the parent impinges on how they relate to the world in every way. The attachment relationship provides a 'secure base' (Bowlby 1969) from which the teenager can explore and master the world. In contrast, teenagers who have an insecure attachment relationship with their parents trigger excessive levels of stress chemicals which, coupled with the surge of teenage hormones, can easily tip the teenager into persistent states of irrationality and frustration or indeed repeated outbursts full of rage and anger.

The relevance of a traumatic childhood to teenage anger

Childhood trauma has a huge impact in terms of difficulties during adolescence. Historically, the general belief was that children are naturally resilient and therefore able to cope with traumatic events. However, with new brain scanning technology, a very different and concerning picture has emerged, showing long-term adverse impacts of trauma on the child's developing brain, including shrinkage due to cell death, in key areas concerned with emotional and social intelligence (see Teicher 2002; 2003; 2006).

Childhood trauma can lead to a hypersensitive stress response system in the brain. This means that the teenager then responds to minor stressors as major emergencies, with the body-mind triggering flight, fight, or freeze responses to stressors that others would simply take in their stride. Consequently, teenagers who have been subjected to trauma often find themselves in persistent painful states of hyper-arousal and hyperactivity. The effects of childhood trauma on teenage behaviour are wide ranging and can include:

✳ Rapid regressions in behaviour and shifts in emotional states.

✳ Aggressive behaviours towards self and others.

✳ Poor physiological and emotional regulation (e.g., sleep, food, self-care).

✳ Self-hatred, self-harm and self-blame.

✳ Risk-taking behaviours.

✳ Feelings of utter helplessness.

✳ Troubled relationships.

Moreover, research shows that teenagers of parents who are drug or alcohol dependent face a far higher risk of suffering physical abuse (Geldard & Geldard 2004) as such parents often have poor anger management skills themselves. They become increasingly frustrated by their teenager's challenging behaviour and can resort to violence and abuse as a means of control. Adolescents who have suffered physical abuse can then respond by demonstrating anti-social and aggressive behaviours or they may internalise their problems, and become withdrawn and depressed.

How to Help

Get results through education, not punishment

It is easy to see why people want to punish angry teenagers. However, if you consider what is happening in the teenage brain and body during a raging outburst, one might re-consider whether punishment is the best course of action. When the teenager is enraged, the mammalian and reptilian parts of the brain are activated compelling them to primitive fight, flight or freeze behaviour. Their frontal lobes are flooded by stress hormones and are therefore unable to think rationally or make good choices. Punishment is inappropriate as the young person is in emotional turmoil. It is more appropriate to talk to the teenager at a time when they are not angry, in terms of where they made bad choices and how they might better deal with a similar situation in the future. There should be consequences for unacceptable behaviour but these should not be delivered through shame, put-downs or anger. There should be a communicated understanding that being overwhelmed with rage, and the triggering of the primitive impulses of a threatened animal can be both painful and frightening.

Camila Batmanghelidjh, a true advocate for vulnerable children and founder and director of Kids Company, a national organisation helping thousands of troubled teenagers, explains this further: 'For the traumatised child frozen emotionally by the absence of love and the experience of humiliation, there is a need to take revenge and a storage of hate. Punishment is experienced as rejection, which deepens the child's resentment. The only hope is to find love for this child … once these children feel contained and consistent love they will not want to lose it' (2006).

The impact of extreme anger on adolescent health

While it must not be forgotten that many teenagers feel anger that is justified, excessive anger is very damaging physically, as it places a lot of stress on the body. Some of the costs to physical health can include headaches, stomach aches, exacerbation of asthma and, through the release of high levels of norepinephrine (which narrows blood vessels), high blood pressure. Research (Crist 2008) has found that teenage boys who react angrily to stress were three times more likely to have heart problems. So anger is not something that should be ignored. Considering this impact on physical health, it is clear that teenagers with excessive anger need help.

Why some anger management programmes fail

It is clear that traditional, short-term anger management courses which aim to 'stop' angry adolescents from reacting to situations with aggression and violence have very limited success. Adolescents often refuse to engage with 'some strange counsellor who thinks he knows me', or if they do in fact show interest and engage positively in the anger management course the short-term interventions appear to have no long-term impact on changing behaviours that are so ingrained. This is because for many teenagers anger is used as a defence to make them feel powerful, and so gives them a sense that no one can hurt them as they may have been hurt in the past. They soon learn that people are intimidated by the displays of violence, anger and aggression.

Setting Up Effective Anger Management Programme Within Schools

A residential BESD (Behavioural, Emotional and Social Difficulties) school for boys aged 11 to 17 years identified that many of the teenagers who were being referred had long histories of anger and violence, resulting in numerous school exclusions. Many displayed extreme aggression and violence, directed at staff and other students. 'Anger management' was a phrase that was repeatedly mentioned as a way forward. However, referral to outside agencies took time and such a delay heightened the risk of school exclusion. Often, the behaviour of these young people had already put their school placements in jeopardy. What they needed was more immediate support. The school decided that an 'in-house' anger management programme was needed.

Students were referred to the programme by staff members. I began by meeting three of the teenagers for individual one-to-one meetings, on a weekly basis. The programme went from strength to strength and within three years 27 young people were engaged on the programme – more than half of the school's nominal role.

The anger management programme provided is a structured one, intended to guide and educate teenagers so that they understand the difference between healthy expression of anger and unhealthy anger. The young person begins engagement in the programme through a variety of routes (referral from teachers, social care staff, parents or self-referral). The decision whether or not to engage, however, ultimately lies with the teenager themselves. This type of intervention will only ever be successful if the teenagers want to make changes to their behaviour. Since the service was started only two young people have rejected the support.

The success of the programme has been due to several fundamental reasons. One of these is having a skilled staff team who understand that:

✳ Troubled teenagers are extremely wary of people they don't know. It takes time for them to build up trust in others, as they have often been badly let down by adults in the past.

✳ Many troubled teenagers have attachment difficulties. They may not have been fortunate enough to have a reliable and emotionally available parent who is interested in them, will soothe them consistently when distressed, protect them and help them to attune, contain and soothe when they were frightened, scared or angry.

✳ The troubled teenager's resilience is often low, and anger acts as a useful defence.

✳ Troubled teenagers are often unwilling to meet a stranger to talk about their anger because they do not see their anger as a problem, anger has helped to protect them in the past.

The need for one-to-one sessions on a regular basis

Teenagers are often unwilling to talk to adults about personal or sensitive issues. They may find it too embarrassing and are wary that by describing their difficulties they may become emotionally overwhelmed and consequently vulnerable. If they hold information back, they retain their privacy and avoid the possibility of needing an adult at a time when they are trying to achieve separateness and independence (Geldard & Geldard 2004). However, when a familiar face offers the teenager one-to-one time each week to help them to try to find better ways of dealing with stressful situations, ways that will not get them into trouble at school, at home, or with the law, they are often much more willing to attend.

Colleagues delivering the anger management sessions are familiar faces around the school. The teenager meets with the same member of staff, his 'coach', at the same time each week. The initial programme is intensive; the student attends a fifty minute session each week. Students typically attend eight to ten intensive sessions, depending on their individual working pace and understanding of the themes covered.

One of the important initial discussion points is what triggers the student's anger. Once the student has such awareness, and it has been shared with the anger management coach, they can learn how to avoid these triggers or use better strategies to deal with them. Crucial to the success of the intervention is the coach sharing information with other colleagues. The teenager is fully aware that information will be shared sensitively with other key staff, so that those staff can be more understanding and more able to support the teenager when they encounter situations that trigger feelings of anger or frustration.

Early stages of the anger management programme

Teenagers learn about the importance of healthy anger, and the destructiveness of verbal and physical abuse and violence. They are taught about the origins of anger, how it was an important emotion for our ancestors in staying safe, and how the function of anger in society has evolved through the ages. It is explained that while anger was a means of survival for our ancestors (think cavemen) and may have been important for the teenagers' own survival in the past, it can manifest as dysfunctional abuse or violence which can limit positive opportunities for them in their future life. (Examples of how and why are given.) The importance of acknowledging anger and not bottling it up is explained. They begin to learn that the ways they have expressed their anger in the past are unacceptable and need to be adapted.

The coach explores with the teenager alternative ways of dealing with their anger instead of punching people, smashing windows or self-medicating with drugs and alcohol. Such alternatives focus on exercise, e.g., punching a punch bag, kicking a ball against a wall, going for a run, going for a 'stomp', and individual activities such as skipping or drumming. Students are discouraged from participating in team events when they are angry, as they will inevitably vent their anger on another person (either verbally or physically). The coach takes the time with each teenager to find something that they enjoy, and importantly that helps to release 'pent up' energy (it could be as simple as listening to their favourite music and dancing!).

As well as helping teenagers to release their angry energy, the coach talks about various calming strategies. Wherever possible the teenagers are encouraged to take 'time out', get some fresh air and focus on breathing slowly (breathing in for four seconds and out for seven) and most importantly, when they are ready, to try to talk to a trusted person about what initially may have triggered their anger.

Another calming strategy involves the teenager thinking of someone important to them (commonly they will think of an important family member e.g., their mother or grandmother). What would that person think if they could see them behaving in a violent or abusive manner? Would they be proud of them, or disappointed? The coach refers to these strategies as 'anger blockers'. Other anger blockers include asking the teenagers to remind themselves of their goals – what are they aiming for in life? Would being violent or aggressive take them closer to, or further away from achieving this goal? Students are also encouraged to make a conscious effort to relax tense muscles, as it is the body tensing and hands forming fists that signals the start of the angry outburst. They have the option to follow an alternative path – a calm one, where they are in control of their actions and retain their dignity.

An important aspect of the programme involves educating the teenagers about the effects of excessive anger on the body. Young people are often very surprised that anger can cause so many health problems and have a significant impact on their potential future happiness. It is often at this point that they decide that they really do want to make changes, and will ask for help.

The anger management sessions are delivered in a caring and empathic manner, never shaming the teenager. The developmental changes that take place through adolescence in terms of brain and body development and hormonal changes and how these impact on feelings and behaviour are explained in detail. The coach often talks about the teenage brain and how it is hard for them to resist impulsive reactions and to reflect before acting. Teenagers learn that this is not an excuse for their behaviour. Nevertheless this information really helps them to start to feel 'normal' when they understand that there are reasons why they feel such anger. What a relief, when for so long they may have been labelled 'bad' or a 'problem'. When talking about angry and aggressive behaviours we often use the phrase, 'It's your *behaviour* I don't like, not you'. Teenagers respond positively to this, and begin to understand they may not be bad people, but that their behaviours need to change to enable them to live life well. Most importantly, they do not feel shamed or victimised.

Developing empathic skills

The programme also involves developing emotional literacy skills. The teenagers are made aware that anger often masks other feelings that are more difficult to show, for example: jealousy, sadness or fear. This is especially relevant in the type of school setting discussed because when teenage boys are upset or scared, they tend to strike out in anger, rather than acknowledging their true feelings. Shedding tears or admitting that they are scared is often not an option, punching something or someone, however, can boost credibility. We also aim to encourage teenagers to develop their empathic skills. We talk about peer relationships and ways of recognising whether one of their friends or a member of their class group is experiencing difficulty. Again, this can help young people feel 'normal', knowing that others around them are often struggling with similar problems.

At specific stages on the programme we talk about what to do when others are experiencing difficulties. The students are encouraged to think about what they could do to help, whether they should give the person space, offer advice or let a member of staff know that their friend is having a difficult time. We discuss how the response to another teenager will vary, depending on the individual and the type of relationship that they have with that person, for example, a best friend compared to the new boy in the class. This is an important lesson for young people as they learn to read situations in a more psychologically informed way. They begin to interact more appropriately with others as they start to understand different relationships and social situations. Students are encouraged to start to take responsibility for their actions and begin to accept that there are always consequences to the choices they make, either positive or negative.

Using worksheets and other materials to explain what anger is

Over a period of time the anger management team has developed its own extensive range of bespoke worksheets and materials. These enable the team to address the issues that are specific to the difficulties experienced by the adolescents. The materials have been produced in response to regular evaluations of the programme, listening to the feedback that the teenagers provide, and recognising the issues that frequently arise in sessions. These materials are visually appealing, but more importantly, they are concise and informative about specific adolescent issues. We explain to the students that the worksheets are used to help to explain what anger is. In response there is usually a loud groan! However, once they see the worksheets, and begin to work through them, their interest is often sparked.

Follow-up sessions to consolidate learning

After the initial intensive course, the student is offered shorter, weekly meetings for as long as they need to attend. During these sessions, topics covered in the initial intensive course are revisited, and opportunities are provided to talk through any difficulties that may have arisen over the past week, should they want to. This is where the importance of the relationship between the teenager and their anger management coach becomes increasingly evident. Providing the teenager with consistency through regular meetings, held at the same time with the same person is crucial, especially when the attachment difficulties of these vulnerable young people are considered. The meetings provide opportunities to return to strategies, themes and psycho-educational points that may not have entirely resonated in the initial programme. Among these could be the possible reasons behind propensity to anger and aggression, the effects of medication, drugs and alcohol on thoughts, feelings and behaviours, the effects of diet and exercise on general wellbeing and mental health and the developing teenage brain.

The coach works on the premise that teenagers benefit from repetition of information. I believe this is a key strength of the programme. Many teenagers attend more than thirty sessions. It is not uncommon to find that in one of the later sessions they suddenly grasp a concept that was introduced in one of the very first meetings. This highlights the need for repetition when working with teenagers. The meetings also provide the opportunity to practise and role-play situations, so rather than simply discussing good strategies the teenagers can physically practise them, as many times as they need to. We have found that this practice means that the young person is more likely to employ positive strategies when faced with anger triggers in their lives.

One-off crisis management sessions

Occasionally, 'crisis management' sessions are held with students following an 'explosion' of anger. They are given the opportunity to talk through what happened, stage by stage, and we help them to find a solution. During these sessions students tend to 'self-counsel' by using a 'Rage Gauge' to measure the intensity of their anger. They reflect on the appropriateness of their response to the stress trigger and what stopped them from implementing the newly learned strategies. These sessions are always extremely valuable. They are able to reflect on their own behaviour and recognise what they would try to do differently should they find themselves in a similar situation again.

Students are given the opportunity to 'rewind' a situation, like a film, and propose a possible 'script' of action that would have had a more positive outcome than the one they chose originally. As a result of using this technique, we have found that the teenagers are often far more willing to consider changes that they could make in the future, than if they had simply been lectured to by a well-meaning member of staff.

A written personal strategy plan

Communication is considered to be hugely important in the success of the anger management programme. At the end of this intensive course, a Personal Strategy Plan is produced in conjunction with the student. Each plan is available electronically on the staff computer network (with the teenager's agreement). This is crucial; it raises awareness among all of the staff (teachers, care staff, matron and the management team) of each student's triggers, anger style and agreed strategies. Many young people have reflected that this sharing of information is a relief. Sometimes they talk about issues that they find extremely difficult during sessions. They often want people to be aware of their difficulties, but find telling many different people is just too hard.

Therapeutic Arts-Based Counselling as an Alternative or Addition to the Anger Management Programme

This school-based anger management programme has proved to be a very successful intervention in its own right. However, it still really only addresses the 'symptoms' (violence, aggression and fighting) rather than the roots of the behaviours. The success of the intervention is often limited if the cause of the anger is not being addressed. Therapeutic arts-based counselling helps some teenagers to acknowledge, recognise and name the feelings fuelling their anger and gives an opportunity for catharsis. The overall aim of such therapy is to offer a deep understanding of the teenager's emotional experiences, past and present, validating their needs and feelings, laying the foundation for repairing the failures of previous relationships.

Unless negative early life experiences are worked through they are all too likely to surface again in some form during the teenage years. Very often this is seen in the form of primitive fight, fight freeze responses to stresses that other people would simply take in their stride. Therapy aims to empower the teenager to work through their painful early life experiences, undergoing the necessary grief work. As a result, their past will be less likely to spoil the present and future.

Art as Therapy

Traditional 'talking' or cognitive therapies can often be difficult for adolescents. The therapeutic use of the arts is an effective alternative approach to facilitating communication with young people. In *Playing and Reality* Donald Winnicott (1971) writes, 'It is in playing and only in playing that the individual child or adult is able to be creative and to use the whole personality, and it is only in being creative that the individual discovers the self'.

Therapeutic use of the arts offers a powerful way for the teenager to speak about his 'inner world' (a private world of on-going thoughts, feelings and perceptions). Parts of the self that were never 'allowed' in the past and may have been buried, hidden and left without a voice may surface through their play. When approached in the correct manner therapeutic use of the arts can be very permissive, enabling the teenager to explore, experience and express their 'forbidden' feelings. As anger can trigger such an intense emotional discharge, it can be scary. A huge advantage of using the arts for therapeutic conversation with a teenager is the way in which an image, painting, sandplay or clay sculpture can act as a container for feelings that may have previously felt overwhelming. The arts can help to contain powerful feelings such as hate, rage and distress, promoting a sense of safety for the teenager around feelings that may previously have been too scary to even acknowledge.

The following three case studies demonstrate some of the ways in which the arts can be used therapeutically. All names have been changed to protect confidentiality.

Case Study Using Puppets – Zach (age 14)

Zach often chose to use puppets to communicate his feelings. This allowed him to tell me about relationships that had been hurtful and abusive. As he grew to realise that these relationships were fundamentally wrong, Zach also started to realise that his anger was justified. He began to feel safe enough to show me this anger in his play with the puppets – showing what he would like to say (and do) to the abusive adults. I am confident that this feeling of safety was due in part to the relationship that we built up; it was also increased by knowing that should his play threaten to overwhelm him; he could simply remove the puppet and thereby remove himself from the situation, only revisiting the issue again when he felt able to. The puppets provided the containment.

Case Study Using Sandplay – Robert (age 12)

The sand tray as used in sandplay therapy is another extremely effective container for feelings. Adolescents often create scenes of destruction and violence using sand, their play involving fighting and war. This has been hugely revealing to me as a therapist, enabling me to have a glimpse of their inner world. The sand tray provides adolescents with the opportunity to explore the volcanoes, the eruptions, the warring in their world, in a safe and contained manner. Robert had language difficulties and by using sand he was able to show me what life was like for him (past and present) without having to overcome the obstacle of finding the right words to express himself.

Case Study Using Clay – Henry (age 16)

Clay is also very useful when working on anger. One example of its effectiveness occurred when I was working with Henry, a teenager who was talking about a recent bereavement. Discussing the issue stirred up emotions related to bereavements he had experienced in the past. He became quite restless and said that he was beginning to feel angry. I told him that it was normal to feel angry with such painful life circumstances, but that he needed to express his feelings in a safe manner. I suggested using clay. He spent the remainder of the session throwing large lumps of clay at the floor as hard as he could. I encouraged him to shout his pain as he did so; initially, he was a little reluctant but as I showed him what I meant he quickly joined in – trying to shout louder than I could. At the end of the session he began laughing and commented that the lumps of splattered brown clay on the floor 'Look like shit!' He then went on to say 'It's a bit like life sometimes, but it feels better when the shit is out in the open, rather than building up inside me'.

I was taken aback, his reflection perfectly embodied the true aim of therapeutic engagement with these young people; being by their side and supporting them while they work through and try to make sense of their 'shit'.

Conclusion

Therapeutic work with teenagers can be tough, stressful, heart-breaking and frustrating, yet hugely rewarding when you get through. Anger, in particular, presents particular challenges as it can take real courage to confront, both for the individual and for the witness. The school-based interventions discussed in this chapter were introduced and delivered with a common aim; to educate teenagers about their anger and to show that the healthy expression of anger is hugely important. The reasons for the success of the interventions are summarised below:

✳ Teenagers are provided with the psychological knowledge regarding:

- Possible roots to anger (the neurobiological and environmental causes), and the 'safety' that anger can provide as a defence mechanism.

- The negative impact that extreme anger can have on the body and the mind.

- The fact that anger is not a negative emotion, in some forms it can be healthy and vital.

✳ Teenagers who have fully embraced the support offered by the programme, demonstrate an increased ability to regulate difficult emotions. They become more aware of, and familiar with, their own anger style and are introduced to different ways of coping with frustrating situations. The adults delivering this support are crucial because they remain alongside the teenagers during sessions, week-in week-out as non-judgemental, caring and empathic adults, offering guidance regarding different behavioural 'choices'.

✳ The programme is flexible, giving the most appropriate support for each teenager, either in the form of a structured anger management programme or therapeutic use of the arts.

✳ Open and honest communication between staff members about the adolescent's individual emotional needs and emotional journey has proven to be vital, always with the intent of providing support and care.

✳ Finally, the availability of support to students has been at the core of the success of this intervention. The staff members delivering the sessions are familiar faces, working in the school on a full-time basis. Teenagers have easy access to these trained staff members, who offer consistent and non-judgemental input. The intervention has been cited by many of the young people as making a real difference to their lives and being far better than interventions they have been offered in the past. They often say that for the first time, they feel in control of making *positive* changes to their behaviour and remarkably in many cases they go on and do just that.

Bibliography

Batmanghelidjh C. (2006) *Shattered Lives*, Jessica Kingsley Publishers, London.

Batmanghelidjh C. (2009) 'Terrorised and terrorising teenagers: the search for attachment and hope', in Perry A. (ed.), *Teenagers and attachment; Helping adolescents engage with life and learning*, Worth Publishing, London.

Berne E. (1966)*Transactional Analysis in Psychotherapy*, Grove Press, New York, NY.

Bowlby J. (1969) *Attachment*, Basic Books, New York, NY.

Crist J. (2008) *Mad: How to deal with anger and get respect*, Free Spirit Publishing, Minneapolis, MN.

Geldard K. & Geldard D. (2004) *Counselling Adolescents*, Sage Publications, London.

Giedd J., Blumenthali N., Jefferies N., Castellanos F., Liu H., Zijdenbos A., Paus T., Evans A. & Rapoport J. (1999) 'Brain development during childhood and adolescence: a longitudinal MRI study', *Nature Neuroscience*, Vol. 2 (10), online.

Klein M. (1957) *Envy and Gratitude: A Study of Unconscious Sources*, Tavistock Publications, London.

Luxmoore N. (2006) *Working with Anger and Young People*, Jessica Kingsley Publishers, London.

Panskepp J. (1998) *Affective Neuroscience*, Oxford University Press, Oxford.

Spinks S. (2002) 'Adolescent Brains are Works in Progress: Here's Why', Frontline, Program #2011 www.pbs.org/wgbh/pages/frontline/shows/teenbrain/etc/script.html.

Sunderland M. (2003) *Helping children locked in rage or hate*, Speechmark Publishing, Milton Keynes.

Teicher M.H., Anderson S. & Polcari A. (2002) 'Developmental neurobiology of childhood stress and trauma', *The Psychiatric Clinics of North America* Jun; Vol. 25(2): 297–426.

Teicher M.H., Andersen S.L., Polcari A., Anderson C.M., Navalta C.P. & Kim D.M. (2003) 'The neurobiological consequences of early stress and childhood maltreatment', *Neuroscience and Biobehavioral Reviews* Jan-Mar; Vol. 27(1–2): 33–44.

Teicher M.H., Samson J.A., Polcari A. & McGreenery C.E. (2006a) 'Sticks, stones, and hurtful words: relative effects of various forms of childhood maltreatment', *The American journal of psychiatry* Jun; Vol. 163(6): 993–1000.

Teicher M.H., Tomoda A. & Andersen S.L. (2006b) 'Neurobiological consequences of early stress and childhood maltreatment: are results from human and animal studies comparable?', *Annals of the New York Academy of Sciences* Jul; 1071: 313–23.

Van der Kolk B.A. (2003) 'The neurobiology of childhood trauma and abuse', *Child and adolescent psychiatric clinics of North America* 12: 293–317.

Van der Kolk B.A. (2009) 'Developmental trauma disorder: towards a rational diagnosis for chronically traumatised Children', *Prax Kinderpsychol Kinderpsychiatr.* 2009; Vol. 58(8): 572–86.

Winnicott D.W. (1965) *The maturational process and the facilitating environment*, International Universities Press, New York, NY.

Winnicott D.W. (1971) *Playing and Reality*, Tavistock Publications Ltd, London.

www.pbs.org/wgbh/pages/frontline/shows/teenbrain/interviews/todd.html

www.neurosci.nature.com http://www.nature.com/neuro/journal/v2/n10/pdf/nn1099_861.pdf (November, 2010)

Yurgelun-Todd D. (2002) 'Inside the Teen Brain', Frontline interview on PBS.org.

Life-Story Work Using the Arts

Louis Sydney

This chapter explores the use of life-story work with troubled teenagers and how the use of art media in life-story work can be very effective in terms of the healing process. A case study illustrates how life-story work can get through when other interventions have had little success. Life-story work is a way of enabling troubled teenagers to explore their thoughts, feelings and experiences in relation to their past, present and future. It can encourage them to be proactive and an 'author' of their own story. It offers an opportunity to develop greater meaning.

In making the transition from adolescence to young adulthood, if you have had a difficult start in life, it is so important to have a *coherent narrative* about your life. This means that you have a story about your life that makes sense, a story in which there are no significant gaps or defensive avoidance of any key life events. We know avoidance means that trauma or loss do not get resolved and properly worked through. This often results in debilitating emotional baggage, manifesting in problems with depression, anxiety and aggression. In contrast, life-story work can make that vital difference, enabling the teenager to move into adulthood able to use life well. Furthermore, when a teenager works through their life story with an empathic adult, it can bring about a deep personal connection with that adult.

Life-story work can also help to explain (normalise) or put into context why the teenager is behaving, feeling, perceiving reality in a particular way in the present. It can also bring the teenager a deep sense of relief from sharing what they may, for a long time, have felt to be unshareable.

How to Engage Teenagers in Life-Story Work

Creative arts media such as poetry, lyrics, music, photography, film, mask making, art, sand trays and puppets can all provide valuable ways of better understanding a teenager's internal world. By using these media there is a less confrontational dynamic between the adult and child because there is less of a focus on words. To a degree, the attention moves away from the teenager and the adult and focuses instead on the art image.

Some teenagers are delighted to engage in these activities and means of expression. However, there can be times when arts media such as art ('I can't draw'), drama ('I was no good at it') or music ('Banging on drums is for kids!') can evoke negative memories in teenagers who find the idea babyish or feel that they are involved in something that is not relevant to them. It is therefore important to consider how life-story work can be made more relevant, meaningful and engaging as a process.

For many teenagers, life is all about image. By engaging with what a teenager is currently interested in, an opportunity for a heightened connection is created. By being curious and exploring their lives and interests in a broader cultural sense; asking what they watch on television, film or the internet, what they play on the computer, how they use their mobile phones (what 'apps' they have), who or what inspires them and where they 'hang out', can all be utilised in their life-story work. I would like to emphasise that I am by no means a 'techie' and have no particular interest in technology, but the following examples simply show how a willingness to be open to and curious about what each teenager is interested in can make the difference between engaging with that teenager – or not. Lastly, the willingness of an adult to simply *think* about the teenager and wonder what underlying emotions may be fuelling their presenting behaviour is also therapeutic.

Points to Keep in Mind when Working with a Teenager's Life-Story Work

Age and developmental stage

It is not unusual to find that some troubled teenagers have experienced some form of trauma, neglect and deficit of care. With this in mind, it is helpful to compare the actual age of a child to their developmental and emotional age. For example, a 14-year-old who has experienced abuse and neglect may well be functioning at a much younger age emotionally or developmentally.

Trauma: 'The elephant in the room'

When working through a teenager's life story, professionals can be confronted with the dilemma of how and whether to include or address events that have been traumatic and upsetting in the teenager's past. This is usually due to a lack of confidence on the part of the adult. If a teenager has already lived through the traumatic experience they are entitled to support that makes sense of that experience and helps to put it into some sort of context. Without this they can be haunted by their experiences with hyper-arousal, hypervigilance and mental health problems in terms of aggression, anxiety disorders or depression. As Freud (1909) said, 'A thing which has not been understood inevitably reappears; like an unlaid ghost it cannot rest until the mystery has been solved and the spell is broken'.

Traditionally, life-story books for adopted children or those in care, where life had been chaotic, crazy, incongruent and full of gaps, did not include enough content that was meaningful. Again, this was often due to the adult protecting *themselves* from what might be revealed. The irony is that the teenagers have survived the frightening and abusive environments and often know all too well how difficult their lives have been. Now they need the adult to 'survive it' too. Any silence on the part of the listening adult in terms of the teenager's early life history can only compound the innate shame and fear that teenagers may experience when daring to explore their lives.

> The very fact that adults hesitate to share information about the past with a child implies to him that his past is so bad that he won't be able to cope with it. Whatever the past was, the child lived through it and survived and so he can live with the truth. [That said] the truth can be presented in a harmful way that lowers the child's self-esteem or in a way that helps the child to understand and accept his past and thus raises his self-esteem.
>
> *(Fahlberg 1981)*

Any avoidance or minimising of a teenager's experience of loss or trauma only perpetuates unexpressed pain and conflict in their life. By being able to help the teenagers to reflect on their painful life experiences, adults can enable them to gain a far better sense of how their painful past and troubled present fit together.

Preparation of resources and art materials

Ensure that you have a wide range of materials including paint, crayons, oil pastels, pencils (don't forget an eraser and sharpener) and charcoal sticks. If you have any prior knowledge of the teenager, through previous work or access to reports or files, then some careful thought about how to engage them in the process is important. If you are working with a teenager then discovering what games, activities and interests they like may offer better possibilities for a good connection between you at the start. For example, many comic book heroes have suffered trauma which can be used as a point of identification for a young person, and there are countless super-heroes whose parents have died, been killed or are absent.

Many young people (interestingly, of all ages) respond positively to decorating and shaping dolls houses into representations of their lives or an aspect of their life. They can design a room to represent the past and other rooms to represent life now and in the future. In one case, a child made an improvised basement to represent her past and the 'hell' that she had lived through with black walls, faeces on the floor and a broken smelly bed.

Creating a safe space

Teenagers naturally benefit from being in a safe, nurturing environment when doing life-story work. By giving careful consideration to ensuring that a room is comfortable, free from intrusion (including distracting noise) and *predictable*, a teenager will be more able to focus on the work to hand. The room should embody the qualities of good maternal care: predictability, safety, structure, consistency, nurturing and an adult who can really listen and form a meaningful connection with the teenager. Many teenagers from troubled backgrounds have over-sensitive stress response systems in their brains, so even a simple change of room can evoke anxiety or sensory discomfort as he or she adjusts to the different sights, sounds, textures, smells and heat of a room.

The following case study explores work with a teenager where a more creative approach was needed. It became clear that this particular boy was not able or willing to engage in a straight-talking session about his past. If pushed this would result in arguments between him and his foster carers.

Case Study – Billy (age 13)

I began to see Billy with his foster carer, Sarah, when it appeared that life had become increasingly difficult both at home and at school. Billy was becoming isolated from his peers at school as he continually got into trouble, and at home his foster carer was at a loss as to how to manage his increasingly aggressive and rejecting behaviour. Social Services were worried that Billy might not be able to remain in his placement with Sarah if his behaviour became unmanageable.

Sarah had identified that after a recent contact with his sister and following a planned contact with his birth mother (who had not turned up), Billy's behaviour had worsened and during an angry outburst he had shouted at Sarah, 'You always let me down … you're not my mother you know, so don't pretend you are!' After he had calmed down and in his own slightly roundabout way apologised, he asked Sarah, 'Is it true that Sophie [his sister] is going to live with mum again?' And, a little later 'I think mum loves drink more than me … do Social Services know who my dad is?'

Billy's early life history involved terrible neglect, emotional abuse, physical abuse and domestic violence within the family home from which he was removed aged three-and-a-half. He had lived in seven foster homes until he was eight and it was suspected, but not proven, that he had been sexually abused in one of these placements. He had lived in his current placement longer than anywhere else in his life yet this now was at serious risk. It was thought that Billy's earlier statement about Sarah not being his mother and questions about his life may be the opportunity for some further life-story work, although Billy's only other such work had been being presented with a life-story book when he was four years old. A social worker had explored the possibility of contact with his birth father, yet it was soon acknowledged that his birth mother was unsure as to the identity of Billy's father.

In our early sessions, Billy was clearly very anxious and presented in an aggressive, rejecting way, letting me know in no uncertain terms how 'boring' it was to visit me. Billy also had a very playful way about him that was most evident when he perceived that he was in control. He clearly did not like novelty and struggled with spontaneous play initiated by another, which is not uncommon for children who have experienced severe trauma or neglect. It was also clear that his foster carer adored him more than she was frustrated by him. However, she was also aware of being physically frightened by him at times, as he was big for his age. It was a regular occurrence for Billy to swear at his foster carer, throw objects at her and on three occasions he had kicked her.

When we started being together he quickly became bored when attempts were made to explore any of the issues related to his early life history. He would put his hands over his ears and shout, 'Blah, blah, blah, blah, blah!' and slide onto to the floor and hide himself under cushions. However, as we progressed and I talked about what I knew about his early life he started to listen. At one point, I wondered aloud whether the recent statement from his sister saying that she was going to live with his birth mother had made him feel 'left out'. He became sad and nodded. Further exploration also confirmed that he was worried about her as well. He believed that she would be let down once again by their birth mother and would not be able to stay. I also suspected that there were unexpressed feelings of sibling rivalry between Billy and his sister but thought we could address these at a later date.

I validated his feelings of sadness and anxiety and empathised with his experience of conflict and he began to become thoughtful without being defensive. I took this opportunity to mention to Billy in a matter-of-fact way that our work together might help the muddled feelings he had about his birth family if he were to bring his life-story book to the next session for us to look at together.

Billy did bring his life-story book to the next session and almost threw it at me, saying, 'There! If you want to read it sometime!' I invited him to sit with me and Sarah sat with us as well. The life-story book appeared to be set out in a fairly traditional way, in that it had photographs of the hospital in which he was born, a photograph of his birth mother smiling with the father of Billy's sister, a picture of a his birth mother cutting his birthday cake when he was four years old at a contact centre (with a caption saying 'Mummy Jane celebrating your 4th birthday …Happy Birthday Billy!'). There were also pictures of various foster carers and their homes with Billy offering a grimaced smile in many of them. I took my time and was curious about many of the pictures exploring what he could or could not remember. I decided to take a risk, saying:

'Oh! Do you know what?', as I leafed through the pictures.
'No…what is it?' Billy looked baffled.
'There's something missing!'
'What?' he asked.
'I can see the pictures of where you were born, your birth family home, your mum in the lounge … but I can't see any pictures of the poo on the floor, mouldy food on the table, dirty mattresses with strangers sleeping on them or police bashing into the house after yet another argument.'
Billy looked at me incredulously and asked, 'How do *you* know?'

I told him that his social worker had shared some information, Sarah had shared some as well and I began to draw some images and words that came to mind which represented his early life trauma, saying, 'This is what I know about you …'

I drew stick figures fighting, children eating excrement as they were starving, strangers sleeping in the house, syringes on the floor, dogs barking, etc. Billy was transfixed by the process, entering what appeared to be a state of receptivity and engagement and commenting that I should add 'Old milk for the children to drink that even made the dogs puke and sometimes I slept on poo in my cot'.

This process also allowed for some reflection where a deeper level of meaning could occur by a mutual agreement that his early life trauma both illustrated and made sense of his current behaviour and therefore *normalised* his aggression. My empathic response towards Billy's adapted and learned aggression enabled him to begin to re-frame his personal story and beliefs about himself.

I suggested to Billy that we explore and think about his life story again but this time in more depth, and in a way that meant he could ask any question he liked and could wonder aloud about things he may have never dared to think about properly before. He agreed.

For the next session, I had prepared a number of printed A4 photographs depicting a combination of nature scenes, people showing different feelings in their facial expressions, urban homes in disrepair and a number of record album covers (these can portray interesting and challenging graphic images). I asked Billy to look at the images spread out on the floor and to choose those that interested him, those he felt drawn to or ones that represented in some way what life had been like for him at home with his birth mother. I was impressed at the responsive way Billy rapidly gathered images and systematically laid them out in a chronological format. I then asked him to provide me with a 'show and tell' about what he had chosen.

What followed was a very moving, poignant and coherent description of his early life trauma. His description was quite matter-of-fact, yet clearly at the same time carried a tangible sadness. It was a relatively straightforward process to get Billy to recreate his life story on a long piece of wallpaper lining. Working together, we created a timeline using words, drawn images and the photo images he had chosen from the floor. We began exploring what had happened to his parents before he had been born. It was clearly evident that he felt relieved to hear that his parents had always fought and argued, dispelling the perception that it was somehow *his fault* that his birth parents had been so violent towards one another.

We included all the more difficult material about his early life history, such as dog poo on the floor, strangers coming into the house and sleeping in his bed, mouldy food in the fridge and his sense of going for a walk along a local street without supervision at an early age.

When we explored this chaotic period of his life, I asked him if he may have felt 'Anything like this?' and I scribbled on the paper with three crayons in my hand, making a whirl of intense, dark colour. Billy joined in and added two more dark colours. When he had finished, he spat on to the picture and as I acknowledged the depth and darkness of his feelings, he rubbed the spit onto the picture, blending it into the artwork.

The timeline work progressed to the point in his personal history when he left his birth family and began a series of different stays in foster care. I invited Billy to choose various toy figures to place upon the timeline to represent different people. He chose toys and figures to represent his birth parents, himself as a baby, the police, social workers, tin cans, syringes and a bloodied bandage. Billy clearly felt sad and looked thoughtful when thinking about his foster carers, yet in a way that seemed totally appropriate to what was being explored. It was a pleasure to see him almost physically expand as he thought about how he had first met Sarah, his current foster carer. Everyone involved in the life-story work agreed that trying to settle in with Sarah had challenged Billy to his core and he admitted that he had felt threatened and frightened at the thought of feeling dependent or vulnerable with Sarah.

Billy was soon ready to explore his many feelings about being taken into care. I invited him to choose a colour for each feeling he could think of and then paint his hands and place them on any areas of the timeline that somehow matched those feelings with that particular time. Billy chose:

✳ Blue – to represent his sad feelings.

✳ Black – to represent his despair.

✳ Red – to show his angry feelings.

✳ Purple – to represent hope in his life, particularly with Sarah.

✳ Green – to represent his happy feelings.

Sarah was also invited to do the same and this clearly had an impact on Billy as he saw how sad, tearful and angry Sarah felt about how he had been mistreated in his early life.

When he returned for the next session, Billy wanted to see his timeline once more. He had photocopied his birth certificate and wanted to stick it on his work. It seemed in some ways as though he was able to integrate and reclaim his early life trauma as *his* story rather than a sequence of events that had happened to him.

Billy then wrote letters (which were not to be sent) to his birth mother and father. Like many children he was not entirely sure what to write, say or ask initially, yet when provided with a basic structure and support that allowed him to reflect, he soon became engaged with the task. At first, he needed to think about beginning the letter and how he wanted to start. In this case, he was very sure that he simply wanted to start with the mother's name. Billy continued his letter with a number of questions:

Mum …
'Why didn't you look after me?'
'I want to know if you still think about me?'
'Do you have any more children and have you hurt them like you did me?'

To help him express himself more fully I began to suggest a number of narratives:

✳ A thing that I remember that made me happy with you was…

✹ A sad memory I have about you is…

✹ Something that was scary was…

✹ One thing I feel angry about was…

✹ One thing I can't forget about you is…

✹ One thing I always wanted to ask you was…

✹ One thing you never understood about me was…

✹ One thing I never understood about you was…

✹ If I could change one thing it would be…

✹ I have to let you know that…

✹ The way I want to end this letter is…

My experience has been that if a particular sentence starter holds no interest for the young person, he or she will simply want to move on to the next one. In Billy's case, he found the letter to his birth mother much easier to write than the letter to his birth father. He was surprised by this and yet a little exploration revealed an unspoken longing for connection with a father he had never known and he shared a fantasy (common among many children who are in care or adopted) that his birth father would one day come and rescue him from his life, take care of him and make things better. The process of writing a letter to his father moved Billy into a period of 'adaptive grieving'. This process is described by Brodzinsky (2004) as 'when a child (often between 8–10 years of age) begins to realise what relinquishment means'.

Having written the letters, Billy was helped to create two life-size dummies using only paper masks and old clothes from a charity shop (stuffed with cushions) to represent his birth parents. At the end, they looked immensely lifelike and Billy was encouraged to pay specific attention to adding the detail of any particular physical aspects of his birth parents such as scars, tattoos, moles and make-up.

When the letters were completed, Billy was invited to read each of them to the birth parent dummies. Sarah read her own letters to them to show Billy how to do it and also to express her feelings about what had happened to him. In preparation for this exercise, Sarah had been supported to rehearse and speak with real feeling and emotion when reading her letters. The process was incredibly powerful and moving and by the end of the session, both Billy and Sarah left the room hugging each other tightly. It had been especially moving for Sarah to witness Billy voicing his feelings in a way she had never seen before (at least in such an emotive, positive and coherent way). After a break, we thought about what to do with the birth parent outlines. Billy wanted to be involved in taking them apart, bagging them up and putting them in the bin. I offered him the option of taking photographs of them before they were dismantled.

A cautionary note: It is important to be mindful of structuring this process. It is not unusual for children to get over-excited and then want to physically attack the dummy figures, hence the need for some reflective time to think and create a plan for how to take them apart. By attacking the figures in an unstructured way, the session may progress in an unhelpful uncontained way. The creation of a holding and containing environment is paramount at all times. A straightforward approach that dissuades the teenager from damaging the dummies is usually enough to help them to manage any left-over feelings of anger.

As Billy was supported to think about this work, it was suggested that he create an music playlist to describe his early life history and time in care. I had hardly finished my sentence before he began reciting the songs he could think of and for the final session a CD landed on my lap to be played. He'd entitled it 'Angry boy tunz! ' A specially made CD cover was the last thing he attached to this piece of life-story work.

At the completion of the life-story work Sarah reported that Billy had played his CD frequently and had begun to talk regularly to her about his life-story work. Their attachment had clearly grown stronger and although Billy could still be challenging in his behaviour, he was much more able to allow Sarah to calm him down. Billy was also able to feel remorse at his angry outbursts at Sarah and expressed that a part of him hoped that Sarah could adopt him, as she was the '… only person who had been kind to him and told him that he mattered'.

Conclusions

Life-story work offers wonderful opportunities for exploration into a teenager's thoughts, feelings, experiences and perceptions about his or her past, present and future. Teenagers can use a book, timeline or imagery in the form of a River or Path of Life, even a laptop can be used to create a multimedia integration of film, music, photography and narration. There are a few key points that are worth keeping in mind to support the work:

✳ Ideally, it is (usually) helpful to have a parent or carer involved in supporting the teenager so that the process is held and contained. It is not appropriate if the parent or carer is not a warm soothing, reflective presence. That said, life-story work can be made more meaningful as a co-created narrative.

✳ The room where you choose to do the work needs to be considered and should convey to the teenager that their needs have been thought about. The following points should be considered:

- Is the approach to your building stressful or calming?

- Is your reception area stressful or calming? And is your receptionist warm and welcoming, remember that he or she is the first point of contact.

- Are you able to offer a consistent, safe, predictable room space that is not intruded upon?

- Is there any noise intrusion as troubled or traumatised teenagers are often more vigilant to noise?

- Is the room comfortable and clean?

- Is there anything you need to provide in terms of drink or fruit as part of a nurturing experience?

- Do you have time to offer a 'goodbye' that is not rushed or hasty?

In addition, it is hugely advantageous for professionals to have a simple working knowledge of attachment theory, trauma theory and basic brain science in order to facilitate the work and help the teenager make better sense of their thoughts, feelings, behaviours and body experience.

Life-story work can be thought of as a process of adding 'layers of clarification':

✳ The teenager offers their own perspective of their past and present life.

✳ The parents or carers offer their perspective of what they know about the teenager's life.

✳ File information, medical records, birth certificates, Social Services information should be read to establish the facts about the teenager's life.

✳ Police files and newspaper archives can all offer more to the life-story work.

✳ The professional can help to make sense and review the above information with the teenager.

✳ Use of drawing, play therapy and the arts also help to integrate and develop reflective thinking and add depth to the therapeutic work by using a creative and centrally expressive approach.

In facilitating life-story work, the utilisation of a teenager's interests in terms of culture, media, television programmes, films, sporting interests, fashion, computer games and more, will often provide insight and an opportunity to engage them. For example, one teenager I worked with had little interest in creating a 'family tree' yet became fully engaged when drawing his family members as if they were a football team (the symbols of family members being defenders, midfielders, strikers or substitutes was also interesting!). Another child found it hard to think or write about her early life trauma yet was certainly willing to think about and write scenes about her life in terms of a soap opera or a 'horrible history'.

Life-story work can often be described as both the journey and the destination and it can offer teenagers a guided path that brings them closer to who they really are and who they want to become as well as healing troubled minds.

Bibliography

Brodzinsky D. (2004) *Adoption News* (Spring/Summer).

Fahlberg V. (1981), *Helping Children When They Must Move*, British Association for Fostering and Adoption (BAAF).

Malchiodi C.A. (ed.) *Creative Interventions with Traumatised Children*, Guilford Press, New York, NY.

Siegel D. & Hartzell M. (2003), *Parenting from the Inside Out*, Tarcher Books, Penguin USA, New York, NY.

* I would like to acknowledge the Family Futures Consortium where some of the creative techniques explored in this chapter were first devised and used.

Working with Anger & Rage in Traumatised Teenagers

Lynne Davis

This chapter looks at how feelings of anger and rage in severely traumatised children can affect their brain development and behaviour in adolescence. It explains the essential differences between anger and rage and offers practical advice on how to enable teenagers to confront and come to terms with their anger or rage by defining it and offering them empathic listening and attunement. A case study demonstrates how real progress can be made with a teenager who is full of rage by using creative expression to help release their rage and understand and make sense of the feelings that often lie beneath.

Understanding the Brain Science Behind Anger in Traumatised Children

The importance of recent discoveries in neuroscience and their implications for the treatment of anger and rage in teenagers cannot be underestimated. A basic awareness of neuroscience helps to explain how anger and rage can dominate in traumatised teenagers. Neuroscience and recent brain studies now show us the impact of early abuse and neglect on brain growth and development, and how the brain's stress response systems can become hypersensitive. This results in a teenager reacting to minor stressors as if they were major threats. Fonagy (2003) notes that 'the brain itself is a social organ', meaning that the higher functioning brain (prefrontal cortex), which is responsible for empathy, reflection, thoughtfulness, impulse control, stress regulation and problem solving can only develop optimally as a result of repeated positive relational interactions. So many teenagers locked in anger have not had sufficient positive relational experiences to fully develop this higher functioning brain. The good news is that it is never too late.

On a recent visit to a South African game reserve I witnessed the birth of a blue wildebeest – an amazing privilege. However, what became noticeable very quickly were the hyenas waiting close by, ready to attack. Within minutes of being born the calf was up, on its unstable new legs, the mother nudging it and encouraging it with her nose. After a few tries and a few falls it was able to walk alongside its mother and join the herd. It found protection in the herd but was also ready to run for survival if it needed to. Although human babies are not able to walk or run to get away from 'predators' or perceived threats, psychologically, the brain systems responsible for this survival or trauma response – fight, flight or freeze – are ready to go. Research shows that if these primitive threat systems are repeatedly triggered in childhood, the child can grow up with vulnerability for depression, anxiety disorders or problems with aggression.

If parents are present and attuned to their babies and children, metaphorically speaking they 'loan' their frontal lobes to the children, making sense of the world for them and putting words to experiences and sensations until the child is able to do this themselves. Therefore a parent or carer's ability to make sense of the world and to regulate their own feelings in turn soothes the baby while they can't do this for themselves. This allows the baby's brain pathways to develop until their frontal lobes are able to take over these functions.

However, if for some reason this process goes wrong and the parent is not able to attune or be empathically present, the child will be left with overwhelming sensory and emotional experiences that they are not able to make sense of or regulate. As a result they may simply cut themselves off from their emotional pain. A famous attachment study showed that children who were left in hospital without their parents or with minimal visits from parents and without a substitute attachment figure, moved from protest to despair and finally to emotional detachment. They tried to cut off from their painful feelings after finding no attachment figure they could turn to for comfort (Robertson 1963). Traumatised teenagers have often had to cut off from feelings from early childhood, as there has been no one there to emotionally regulate them at the time of the trauma. As a result they have limited capacity to reflect, manage stress well and process experiences, as being cut off from feelings leaves emotional development at a standstill.

That said, childhood defences against too much emotional pain often fail to hold in the teenage years. This is due to all the hormonal, body, brain and psychological changes. This means that early childhood experiences of terror, abandonment, shame or loss, successfully defended against in childhood, can be triggered in the teenage years, resulting in intense emotional outbursts and turmoil. This can happen without the teenager having any idea about the connection between what they are feeling now and what has happened to them in their past. Their trauma trigger leaves them flooded with stress hormones making them vulnerable to behaviours which are high-risk and destructive, such as self-harm, violent attacks on others or unprotected sexual activities. This is often the moment when referrals to Child and Adolescent Mental Health (CAMH) services occur.

This is a grim picture, but thanks to advances in neuroscience we now have a clearer understanding of how to support these traumatised teenagers.

Case study – Michael (age 14)

Michael was referred because of his anger outbursts and the referrer requested anger management support. Automatically my thoughts turned to what might be happening for this 14-year-old boy in foster care, severely traumatised in his early life. Michael had frequently been destroying his room and was described as being 'out of control' at these times by his foster carers. Just prior to the referral, an incident had occurred which had resulted in the police being called. Following this, Michael had spent all his time in his room and had destroyed his most prized possession, his mobile phone, resulting in him having no contact with his peers who he described as the most important people in his life. He was not really eating and was not participating in any of the activities he usually enjoyed. It sounded as if he was punishing himself. Michael was aware that his placement was at risk as his carers were talking about terminating it. He liked being with his current carers and yet he refused to apologise for his behaviour, becoming more defensive and oppositional when it was suggested he do so.

I agreed to meet Michael but was very clear that I would probably not be offering traditional anger management, as all the research around trauma and the brain gave me a clear sense that it would have been unsuccessful with Michael. I met him at his foster home. He was a physically small and quiet, and clearly moody. Simply offering Michael a time to talk seemed to reach the part of him that was not receiving much time or attention from the adults in his life, and he agreed to meet with me to see what it would be like.

In our initial meeting Michael talked about how tough he was and how he liked to fight. He often sought out physical fights despite his small stature, making him a target for others, both on the street and on the games field. When we explored feelings, he was proud of the fact that he felt his only emotions were anger and happiness and he denied any feelings of fear and sadness.

I asked about his past and he spoke about his mother who had died years before and how he felt responsible for her death. (The actual cause of her death was cancer.) There had been domestic violence in his family home and he used to take his little brother out if he could, so he did not have to witness it. He went on to describe how, after his mother's death, his father began to physically abuse him and his brother. He had never been able to fight back and felt shame for not protecting his brother. Eventually, he did hit back and was put into foster care and 'disowned'. I concluded that unbearable feelings of fear and grief were very much part of Michael's past, although he was not ready to accept this, and that punishing himself for what he perceived was his fault was deep-seated. Violence was part of his life from birth and the very people who should have kept him safe had frightened him and inflicted physical and emotional pain on him.

Michael's anger

Children whose emotional needs have not been met and do not have 'good enough' parents will either do battle with the world or shrink from it (Bowlby 1973). Michael was a soldier and it became increasingly clear that he was full of unprocessed rage. Sue Parker Hall (2009) believes that rage is a combination of unprocessed feelings, whereas anger is a single, pure emotion. This concept of rage was very much my experience of Michael and many of the teenagers I work with who have histories of abuse and neglect. Michael's rage was intense and out of proportion. He responded to stressors which others would take in their stride, with a 'trauma response', a fight, flight or freeze response. Therefore traditional cognitive methods, where we try to talk troubled teenagers out of the responses they are having through different thought patterns, would not have worked. In Michael's case, the prefrontal cortex (the part of the brain responsible for problem-solving and emotional regulation) had not developed well enough, due to a lack of a 'good enough' parent. Michael's rage had become fixed and as he grew up he moved between the roles of helpless victim and powerful perpetrator. Michael was proud of his rage and did not want to change it. He felt untouchable and he was not willing to give it up. Any perception of threat to his power provoked rage.

At times, Michael replayed his past experiences by provoking others in his life to hurt him, so reinforcing his belief that he was fundamentally flawed and deserved to be hurt and abused. He was, at times, punishing himself for the shame he felt about his mother's death and his inability to protect himself or his brother from his father's abuse. Alongside this he was experiencing a complex grief process, having lost the people that society tells us love us unconditionally – his parents. My experience of him was very different from the persona he usually portrayed. In fact, I saw a sad, lonely child before me. It would take time however, before he would be able to own this for himself. The tender, gentle, vulnerable range of feelings were typically perceived by him as weak and stupid.

Although the early life narratives of traumatised children differ, the rage and destruction experienced by these teenagers and ultimately society is mostly the same. They have had just too few soothing and emotionally regulating relational experiences and so they are surviving in the world any way they can, using the primitive fight, flight, freeze responses to handle life's inevitable stressors.

If Michael could feel my compassion, empathy and warmth, which I genuinely felt, I knew there would be hope. I knew my relationship with Michael would be key to the process of change.

For the traumatised child frozen emotionally by the absence of love and the experience of humiliation, there is a need to take revenge and there is storage of hate. Punishment is experienced as rejection, which deepens a child's resentment. The only hope is to find love for this child. The only thing which can return them from the abyss is the capacity to rekindle their ability to feel, by feeling for them. We have to rise above their defences and gently care for them so that the wound of having been abandoned to the experience of violation can be healed. Once these children feel contained and consistent love they will not want to lose it.

(Batmanghelidjh 2007)

Internalised Versus Externalised Rage

It is important to understand the difference between internalised and externalised anger and rage, in terms of the different ways that rage can be felt and how to work with it, what to look out for and when to seek help. A study found that teenagers in an inpatient mental health unit who internalised their rage were more likely to attempt suicide while those who externalised their rage in assaults on others were more likely to turn to substance abuse as a means of coping (Cautin et al 2001).

Michael is a good example of externalised rage, which was directed at objects and other people. This type of rage is highly charged and will often induce fear in the other or the desire to retaliate. This rage is explosive and very risky to others as well as to the teenager themselves who will tend to participate in risk-taking, high-adrenaline activities, for instance, gang-related activities or hitting out at and then running from the police. Externalised rage often results in these teenagers being referred for anger issues as their problems are so obvious.

Internalised rage on the other hand, is far more difficult to detect as often these teenagers appear depressed and apathetic. Their rage is expressed through behaviours such as self-harm, withdrawal and dissociation. For example, one young girl described how she sometimes became so full of rage she wanted to punch someone but instead she turned to cutting herself as a way of managing the rage that she had been told was unacceptable. Deliberate self-harm is a communication of emotion and it is important that careful attention is paid to this communication. This means really listening to the teenager's description of their feelings prior to and after the self-harm and through our own feelings in response to the teenager's self-harm. Internalised anger often goes unrecognised so these teenagers can struggle on without help for far too long. No one recognises the support they really need. When I worked in a young offenders institution this situation was very prevalent and after a period of internalising their anger, these teenagers would strike out. The intensity of their anger was then excessive.

Another possible behaviour that should be explored fully with teenagers is low mood or depression. Tears are often more acceptable than anger or rage in our society, and young girls in particular tend to cry and have low mood while their anger or rage is not talked about and/or denied by the teenager. The tears offer some relief to the pressure building up inside them. So often in these cases, professionals see the low mood but not the internalised anger, and therefore their work is unsuccessful, or worse, they miss the potential risk of suicide in these teenagers.

Looking Behind the Rage: Shame, Loss, Terror and Invisibility

> Severely maltreated children have legitimate anger and often rage, but it is vital for them, in order to function successfully in their family, school, and social group, to learn to redirect and re-channel the anger in ways that do not further compound difficulties.
>
> *(Crenshaw 2006)*

Helping a teenager find expression for authentic anger in the safety of a conversation with an empathic adult, will often enable the teenager to better channel all their passion into creative and not destructive acts, for instance to create art or perform well on the sports field. In my experience, this work about empowering teenagers to find ways of accepting and using their anger in more constructive ways can be very effective. This can be the case even if it is only for the short term.

Anger management using cognitive interventions (for example, where the teenager is given thinking strategies to use when they feel angry, such as counting to ten) are often more successful with teenagers without a history of trauma. They are able to recognise when they are feeling angry, have enough time to think about the possible options for managing the anger and then are able to put these options into action instead of exploding or imploding. In contrast, rage is arguably a more complex response; a combination of unprocessed feelings from early development.

In Michael's case, the possible feelings underlying his rage arose out of feelings of shame, annihilation, terror and loss, yet he had a limited ability to recall exact experiences or articulate the sensations he had. I was alerted immediately at the point of referral when he was described as 'out of control' and 'unreachable' at times; his anger was not 'clean'. When we talked about his rage, Michael noted that he 'saw red' almost instantaneously and went into a 'trace-like state' which came on within seconds. He said he was not 'in himself' at the time of the actual hitting out, it was only after he had lashed out that he suddenly was aware of where he was and what he had done. This experience often occurred when he perceived he was being challenged by others, either physically or emotionally and when he felt that if he did not fight back he would be vulnerable to the other's rage. Often, after hitting out he would be tearful. He was confused by this, again giving me more information about the feelings underneath his rage. The work needed, therefore, was for me to help Michael put words to feelings and bring in his story so that he could integrate how his past was still affecting him.

Rage Fuelled by Shame

Shame in traumatised teenagers is a feeling of one's very 'self' being utterly flawed, defective and worthless. Teenagers who have been severely traumatised often feel a sense of shame, as they truly believe (either consciously or subconsciously) through their experiences that they are bad and unlovable. The teenagers I work with often hide behind a false self, for example, a self full of bravado to prevent anyone from seeing how awful they feel they are. Not surprisingly, such teenagers will defend themselves against shame by using rage. Rage can enable the teenager to feel safe from having their shame exposed.

For others, shame can lead them to want to hide from the world. This is important when thinking about teenagers who are withdrawn, low key, or depressed in school. A shame-prone teenager will often experience low self-esteem in both tasks and relationships. The aim therefore is to work with the teenager to give them positive relational experiences so they develop a different sense of self from the person they believed they were. Achievements at school, home or in social life should be noted and praised by the adults in the teenager's life (this should start at a small level so that it is not too much and therefore denied, or expressed as 'You're just saying that!').

Rage Fuelled by Loss

In Michael's case, his loss, unprocessed and denied, was fuelling his rage. Yet he no longer allowed himself to feel any sadness or pain. Instead, when these feelings threatened to surface, he moved quickly into a fight and flight response. Michael was angry at the loss of his mother, the loss of his life before foster care, the loss of his innocence and the fact that nobody was there for him. Michael's grief had hardened into rage and he experienced images of violence that he wished to inflict on his father or anyone who tried to befriend him, for example, his foster carers. For teenagers who have been severely traumatised in relationships, it becomes easier to hate than to love and easier to push others away through anger than to experience the pain of not being loved again. But teenagers will melt again if met with real concern, empathy and compassion by a consistent genuinely caring adult over time.

Furthermore, adolescence as a developmental stage entails loss in itself – loss of childhood, loss of idealised parents and loss of school and friends as the teenagers move from junior to senior schools and then to college. But for traumatised teenagers the sense of loss is often so profound that they use the only defence mechanisms they know. Having a space to think about the loss and the impact this has had on their lives, is vital to their being able to make sense of the feelings and to embark on the grief work that cannot be avoided if they are to flourish in the world. For some teenagers they can do this work with a trusted teacher, relative or mentor. For others more support may be needed and the use of psychotherapy may be necessary before they feel safe enough to grieve.

Rage Fuelled by Terror

Traumatised teenagers know the experience of terror too well, although initially it is often hard for them to re-connect with this as they have learned ways of cutting themselves off from it, either through dissociation or other means such as self-harm or substance use. Often, the teenager has been the victim of abuse or neglect, which has not only often threatened their physical being but also their emotional self.

For these teenagers, acknowledging terrified feelings can bring with it a sense of being out of control, overwhelmed and even feeling they are going mad. When the abuse has either been perpetrated by a loved one or they have not been protected from abuse by a loved one, they perceive the world as extremely threatening and unsafe. Such terror activates the amygdala in the brain (the survival centre) and the teenager moves into their fight or flight response. I have often worked with young men who are hardened by their experiences of terror and so project this out into the world, getting a sense of satisfaction from terrifying others. They decide they will never again be a victim and so once they find their rage, they find a way of both being in control and feeling safe in the world again. This rage is often expressed with great intensity as it is rage which has been pent-up for years. In Michael's case, when he felt threatened and therefore terrified, he responded with rage just as he had from the day he learned he could hit back to defend himself.

Rage Fuelled by Feelings of Helplessness and Being Unseen

For some teenagers feeling helpless and as if they have no real impact on anyone or anything, or feeling just too unimportant, unnoticed and unseen can also evoke feelings of terror. In Michael's case, he often felt invisible in his foster home. So rage solved all that. It ensured that he was seen and it made him feel powerful. Although the response to his rage was negative it was far better than the complete rejection he had suffered after his father disowned him

It is important to spend quality time each day with a teenager. Really taking the time to listen, empathise and get to know the teenagers so they feel they are 'enjoyed' is vital. By keeping promises made to a teenager and doing the things one agreed to do, they will feel 'held in mind.' This is key to anyone's sense of self- worth.

What Works? Practical Solutions to Enable Teenagers to Confront and Come to Terms With Their Anger or Rage

Defining the anger or rage

The most important support for any work with teenagers locked in rage and anger is an understanding of the feelings that lie beneath. As Sue Parker Hall (2009) says, 'anger needs to be expressed while rage needs to be transformed'. Simply using anger management for rage – if we take rage to be a combination of unprocessed and denied feelings – means we are missing the teenager's real emotional needs. Bodily arousal must also be considered. Trying to 'talk away' anger or rage through a more cognitive behavioural intervention often leads to a build-up of intense emotional energy and unbearable physiological arousal that can no longer be kept inside. As a result there can be either an explosive outburst or problematic physical symptoms, e.g., frequent illness, self-harm, problems with sleeping, eating, digestion or elimination.

If we think about the emotions *behind* a teenager's behaviour we stand a far better chance of understanding where the fundamental difficulty lies. Knowing as much as possible about the teenager's past is important, so that one can begin to help them make connections between what happened to them *then* and how they are reacting *now*. It is vital that they are helped to make sense of their life narratives. Having information about their key relationships, especially those in their early years with their primary care givers, will enable us to get a sense of the teenager's beliefs about themselves and their relationships to other people. This will also help to assess how brain development may or may not have been affected.

Listening carefully and empathising

> Working with a traumatised child can feel like an assault on your feelings.
>
> *(Batmanghelidjh 2007)*

It is likely that the child professional will, at times, experience in a painful way not only the teenager's cut-off feelings but also their rage. This is particularly the case when the teenager is denying what they feel. For example, Michael's denial of his sadness and fear was fundamental in the work I did with him and I was constantly aware of how keen he was to keep up his defence mechanisms. It would not have been helpful to challenge this directly. Through noticing what I was feeling and empathising with Michael, giving him a sense of how understandable were his responses to his awful life experiences, offered him the permission to eventually explore these 'dangerous' feelings.

Daniel Hughes (1997) has developed a model that addresses attachment and trauma in teenagers locked in anger or hate. His underlying principles are empathy, curiosity, playfulness and acceptance. Being accepting and empathetic is very important but this needs to be directed at the core underlying emotion and not the defence. For example I might say: 'You are really mad today and I can see that in how you are talking. I'm thinking how hard it must have been when you thought that your foster carer didn't care about you'. Empathising with underlying feelings of terror, shame or loss gives the teenager the courage and support to go there too. Always be prepared to be told you are wrong by the teenager and to accept this. You may be wrong, but often when you see through a defence the teenager will feel the need to defend initially, until they feel safe enough not to do so.

Helping Teenagers to Speak About Their Feelings and not Discharge Them in Destructive Behaviours

The ability to put words to the bodily sensations related to different emotional states is often poor in teenagers who are locked in anger or hate. This often results in them being confused by both sensations and feelings. Curiosity and a genuine interest in what is behind destructive behaviours and how the painful past is triggering the teenager in the present can be invaluable. This is known as building a coherent narrative. Linking bodily states with feeling states is also often very helpful to teenagers. For example, I might ask the teenager about how they feel when they are angry. If they don't know I would use myself as an example, saying: 'For me, when I get angry I tend to lock my jaw and become very tense in my shoulders' and then invite them into the conversation with, 'I wonder how it is for you?'

Attunement

Another important aspect of working with teenagers locked in rage or anger is what is described as attunement. This means matching the emotional tone of what the teenager is saying. With angry teenagers, one needs to up the pitch and pace of one's voice and become more animated in line with their emotional energy. This can result in the teenager feeling really met where they are. By matching their energy through attunement, the teenager gets the message that their anger is valid as a feeling, and they are really being listened to. It is often only then that they can calm down and so regulate their level of arousal. After acknowledging the anger or rage in this way, the underlying emotions also need to be attuned to, so that the teenager can work through what needs to be addressed. Attunement is a key factor in the teenager being able to develop well-functioning emotional regulatory capacities in the brain.

Using the arts to help teenagers reflect on their feelings

Using clay, painting, sandplay and music to discuss difficult emotional experiences with teenagers can support them to contact their feelings in a safe and interesting way.

One young girl I worked with was angry at her situation of being in care and had hit out at another teenager who referred to this fact. When I saw her, her rage at being taken from her birth mother was intense. I offered her the image of anger as being like a volcano saying, 'Sometimes some people's volcanoes are bigger than others'. She immediately felt understood and joined me in the image, elaborating on the volcano's size and explaining how she felt about it. In the following session I started to use clay with her as it offered a way of safely releasing angry energy. I asked her to create the volcano using clay. Clay has a very helpful sensory nature, which in turn is very soothing, so her level of arousal came down to a manageable level. Following the creation of the volcano and the release of the energy or bodily tension, it was important to help her talk about her rage and loss. We used a technique called dialoguing, which means she talked 'as if' she was the volcano (also known as giving it a voice). From this, she was able to move into a place of insight. Over time, with similar therapeutic conversations, she never hit out again.

The arts are often very effective at helping teenagers access their true feelings behind a defence of anger. The use of clay, paint or sandplay, for example, offer a way of 'talking about' emotional hurt indirectly and therefore feels safe for the teenager. Michael was not offered traditional anger management because I knew the arts could help him to get to his core feelings. He needed the support of imagination and creativity to override his defences. Through the use of clay and paint he managed to contact his terror and grief. These art media helped him confront his painful past, to the point where it no longer haunted him so much. Using image and metaphor he dared to feel his grief and loss. He was also able to share the loss of his mother through the story of the *Lion King*, which he really identified with.

It is vital that over time defence mechanisms are replaced with adaptive coping mechanisms. Without a way of managing, teenagers are at risk of experiencing again and again the emotional distress from the original trauma, and in so doing reinforcing their view of a harsh hostile world in which their fighting feels justified. That said, it is important to respect the teenagers' rage as a defence mechanism. Often, they feel they would not have survived without it. It will be a sensitive task over time to help the teenager to find healthier ways of coping.

Naturally, a teenager needs to have a strong sense of trust in the adult working with them. Moving too quickly can lead to yet another experience of them feeling frightened by their painful feelings. As part of the process, if we share our knowledge about the brain science of anger and rage, the teenager can feel empowered, realising that they cannot always prevent such intense feelings and that they should not feel shamed by their behaviour. With the knowledge of what is happening in the brain when they are triggered into a state of alarm, the teenager can start to recognise and manage feelings. By knowing that they are not mad or bad, they can start to explore other ways of coping.

Summary

Working with anger and rage in traumatised teenagers is complex and can be challenging for the adults who work with them. How do you stay emotionally regulated, reflective and empathic when the person in front of you has 'lost it'? It is important to bear this in mind when working with these teenagers and ensure that as an adult you get enough support before, during and after any therapeutic conversation carried out with teenagers.

Thinking about which feelings fuel anger and rage is vital if we are to see positive changes in a troubled teenager's behaviour and an ability to live life well. Working to heighten awareness of bodily arousal states, using the arts to access a deeper and more authentic level of feeling, respect for defences and helping the teenager to understand basic brain processes are all key to effective intervention.

Michael still has some difficulties, but he is now able to think about his feelings instead of simply acting them out. He acknowledges his underlying grief and fear as he moves forward in his life. The arts offered him another way of being able to think things through and name experiences that prior to the work remained confusing and deeply troubling. He no longer hits out at the world and the world is no longer as scary for him. He can manage his high arousal states far better. He is aware of his self-worth.

Teenagers with anger and rage need a chance; they need adults in their lives who will listen to them and notice them and then be brave enough to step in and help them so that they can move on and become thriving adults.

Bibliography

Bannister A. (2003) *Creative therapies with traumatized children*, Jessica Kingsley Publishers, London.

Batmanghelidjh C. (2007) *Shattered Lives: Children who Live with Courage and Dignity*, Jessica Kingsley Publishers, London.

Bowlby J. (1960) 'Grief and Mourning in Infancy', *The Psychoanalytic Study of the Child*, Vol. 15: 3–39.

Bowlby J. (1969) 'Attachment and Loss', *Attachment*, Vol. 1, Hogarth Press, London.

Bowlby J. (1973) 'Attachment and Loss', *Separation*, Vol. 2, Basic Books, New York, NY.

Bowlby J. (1988) *A secure base: Clinical applications of the attachment theory*, Routledge, London.

Bradshaw J. (2006) *Healing the Shame that Binds you*, (rev. edn) Health Communications, USA.

Carey L. (ed.) (2006) *Expressive and Creative Arts Methods for Trauma Survivors*, Jessica Kingsley Publishers, London.

Cautin R., Goetz P. & Overholser J. (2001) 'Assessment of Mode of Anger Expression in Teenager Psychiatric Inpatients', in *Adolescence*, Spring issue at www.findarticles. com.

Crenshaw D. (2006) 'Neuroscience and Trauma Treatment: Implications for Creative Arts Therapists', in Carey L. (ed.) *Expressive and Creative Arts Methods for Trauma Survivors*, Jessica Kingsley Publishers, London.

De Zulueta F. (2006) *From pain to violence: the traumatic roots of destructiveness* (2nd edn), Whurr Publishers, Sussex.

Fonagy P. (2003) 'The development of psychopathology from infancy to adulthood: The mysterious unfolding of disturbance in time', *Infant Mental Health Journal*, Vol. 24(3): 212–39.

Geldard K. & Geldard D. (2004) *Counselling teenagers*, (2nd edn) Sage Publishers, London.

Gerhardt S. (2004) *Why love matters: How affection shapes a baby's brain*, Routledge, London.

Hughes D. (1997) *Facilitating developmental attachment: The road to emotional recovery and behavioral change in foster and adopted children*, Jason Aronson Inc., USA.

Morrison A. (1997) *Shame: The underside of narcissism*, The Analytic Press, Hilldale, NJ.

Oaklander V. (2006) *Hidden Treasure: A map to the child's inner self*, Karnac Books, London.

Parker Hall S. (2009) *Anger, Rage and relationship: An empathic approach to anger management*, Routledge, London.

Robertson J. (1953) *A two year old goes to hospital*, [Film] Penn State Audio Visual Services, University Park, PA.

Sunderland M. (2009) Conference on Attachment [*Lecture*], Child Centre for Mental Health, London.

Winnicott D. (1971) *Playing with reality*, Penguin Books, London.

Worksheets & Exercises to Help Teenagers with Anger & Low Self-Esteem

Margot Sunderland

Introduction to the Worksheets & Exercises

These exercises are designed to provide concrete ways and opportunities for teenagers to identify and organise their feelings and ideas about their life experiences, and to form these feelings into communicable statements, either verbal or non-verbal. Sometimes feelings can be very confusing. Teenagers know they feel miserable but don't understand why. Things that have happened in their lives can seem overwhelming and unmanageable.

The exercises are designed to help teenagers to be able to think about their feelings and experiences in a creative way that grabs their attention. This is in part due to the use of illustrations and images. The worksheets demand very little from the teenager. The instructions are often as simple as: 'Tick, colour in or write at the top of a picture which you feel says something about you and your life'.

Seen in the illustration and so objectified, difficult or painful feelings and problems can cease to hold so much power. The illustration is apart from the self, seen from a standing back position, as opposed to a situation in which emotions are experienced as overwhelming or suffocating. Something happens when feelings are worked with actively in a 'doing' pictorial way rather than just a 'thinking' way. Because the exercises are ordering processes, having completed them, many teenagers experience a new clarity of thought. 'I know what I feel' and 'I can explain what I feel' are often accompanied by a feeling of great relief. In addition, clarification of a feeling is often a very important first step to doing something about it.

Moreover, because of the physical presence of the picture, the actual relationship between professional and teenager is also arguably far less threatening than an exchange of words might be. There is literally something between the two of them, the drawing, the shared focus, the third presence so to speak.

Some exercises offer opportunities to rehearse healthier ways of functioning, healthier emotional behaviour, to try out more creative ways of thinking, feeling and being, safely ... on paper. They offer a practice ground to use new skills, and creative ways for dealing with specific emotional experiences, relationship issues and problems. Teenagers can take risks through the exercises, because they offer a safe arena, before having to take the greater risks 'out there'. The exercises can also be used to enable angry teenagers to start to direct destructive energy into more creative channels. This is as a result of all the reflective processes built into the exercises, which are offered in the context of therapeutic conversation with a warm, empathic adult.

Why Not Just Talk about Feelings?

Emotional experiences cannot always be reduced to words. Thinking and talking can interfere with the attempt to get in touch with feelings. The words chosen to convey a feeling may actually very poorly represent that feeling. So by choosing to simply talk about feelings, teenagers often end up feeling misunderstood. Illustrations can help teenagers to 'see' what they cannot verbalise.

The Pictures and Images Used

The pictures and the images in the worksheets are heavily informed by up-to-date psychological research. The teenager doesn't necessarily need to know this, but it does mean that the exercises contain key knowledge about human emotionality, how we suffer and how we thrive. Many of the frameworks are taken from psychotherapeutic concepts, but have purposefully been made palatable and accessible for the teenager.

Furthermore, the great thing about working with teenagers and not children is that, by and large, they are capable of considering sophisticated concepts relevant to the human condition. In fact, they can quickly become fascinated by the psychology behind each of the exercises. Further support is provided to professionals in discussing these tasks by the inclusion of statements and information for a more detailed discussion with the teenager after they have used the worksheets.

Teenagers can be hugely helped to make good decisions in their lives by the psychology offered through the pictures and in the discussion that follows. It is my belief that all teenagers should be privy to the psychological knowledge offered in this section and that it should be a key part of a PSHE curriculum for teenagers. Furthermore, to inform them about what is going on in their brains, when they are feeling rejected, making bad decisions or when they are feeling good, is particularly important at this vital developmental stage.

Themes of the Worksheets & Exercises

The exercises and worksheets are designed to be useful for a wide range of teenagers who are angry for very different underlying reasons and who show their anger in very different ways.

✳ **All about Fighting** – For teenagers who keep getting into fights (p. 125).

✳ **Bullied, Abused, Used** – For teenagers who are angry because they've been bullied, abused or used (p. 139).

✳ **Like a Nightmare Got Stuck in My Brain** – For teenagers who are angry because they've experienced trauma or traumatic loss (p. 149).

✳ **My Relationships Past and Present** – For teenagers who are angry and/or suffer as a result of another person's anger, and because they have experienced too many relationships that have been based on power and control (p. 159).

✳ **The Encouragers & the Rubbishers** – For teenagers who are angry because they've experienced too much shame and discouragement (p. 173).

✳ **Me as Walking Time Bomb** – For teenagers with poor impulse control who lash out when they are angry (p. 187).

✳ **Dog Eat Dog** – For teenagers who are angry because they have been treated with cruelty (p. 199).

✳ **Haunted by Bad Stuff from the Past** – For teenagers who have some awareness that their anger is often over the top because of painful life experiences (p. 213).

All About Fighting

For teenagers who keep getting into fights.

> We are aggressive when we feel threatened.
>
> *(Post 2010)*

Objectives

To help the teenager to step back for a while to consider what fuels their preoccupation with violence. In their own time and when they are emotionally ready, to help to access the feelings of hurt, fear and vulnerability that are inevitably beneath the excitement of, and obsession with, fighting. This will include acknowledging that angry feelings are so much easier to feel than the emotions that lie underneath.

To be informed about what is going on in the brains of people who are often involved in fighting and starting fights and who are fascinated by anything to do with violence, war and fighting. To know and understand the contrast with what is going on in the brains of people who don't want to fight.

All About Fighting

Guidance for the Worksheet

When you feel that your life is so much about fighting you may find it useful to think about it in terms of whether you are happy with carrying on like this or what you might want to change. It can also help to know what makes some teenagers so interested in fighting while others are not interested in it at all.

It might help to think about this with the help of some pictures. So look at the pictures and captions on the worksheet. If any of them show how you feel tick the box or colour in the picture if you like. If how you feel is not like any of the pictures, draw or write in the empty box what you feel inside about the fighting in your life.

All About Fighting

Tired from all the fighting but not able to stop

Fighting makes me feel powerful when I don't feel powerful

Like I've got a war inside me

I want to smash up the whole world

Fighting keeps the pain away

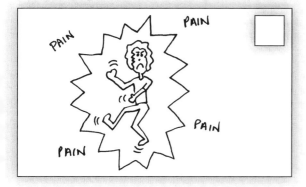

I've known too much war

Fighting keeps my sad feelings away

What to Say to the Teenager

✳ Talk about the brain's natural anti-aggression and anti-anxiety chemicals. (See chapters above). Inform the teenager that for these to be activated we need to feel really safe (physically and psychologically speaking). This means really trusting someone we respect and like to help us.

✳ Talk about how it is important to know the cost when a life is lived focused on the thrill of fighting and violence.

✳ Discuss how it feels when all your energies are taken up in defence and attack with too little energy left over for enjoying life.

✳ It is important to know that painful loss can make people aggressive or violent too.

✳ It can really help teenagers who are suffering in this way to develop heightened awareness of why they are obsessed, thrilled and so excited by fighting. Whenever possible, and when they are ready to hear it, offer empathy for the little girl or little boy underneath the teenager who has such bravado, who has felt very unsafe, desperately alone at times and deeply attacked emotionally and/or physically.

✳ Teenagers by and large benefit from knowing the common origins of this feeling. This often stops them from feeling alone, and hopeless and that they will be feeling like this forever (see below, p. 133).

Talk About ...

... why fighting, war and violence can feel so exciting, sometimes above all else

Sometimes people get hooked on fighting and violent films and games, because these are in some sense a mirror of important aspects of their own lives. They may have been bullied a lot, or seen their parents fighting or arguing frequently, or been hurt with words or been hit by parents, siblings or other children.

They may also have been on the receiving end of too many submission-dominance interactions. This means someone having power over the teenager and them feeling they have no power – rather than having interactions and connections which are about having 'power with'. For example, parents (who often really don't mean it to appear this way) constantly nagging the teenager to do things, and speaking to them mainly in commands and criticism (and not meeting the advised balance of only one negative comment for every six positive ones).

This can make life feel very much like a battle, and so fighting has become a part of their lives. We know from research on violence on television that when people watch these sorts of images, their brains rehearse the violent movements they see.

... the hurt underneath

You could start by saying something along the lines of 'Sometimes people fight physically but what they are actually doing is fighting off a hurt inside them'. For instance, this could be a loss or their parent's divorce.

... powerlessness, helplessness and impotence

You could start a discussion by saying something along the lines of:

'Some people are obsessed with violence and fighting, because at some time in their lives they have known total powerlessness, helplessness and impotence, often in childhood. Fighting gives them a feeling of power and so they turn having no power into a feeling of omnipotence. When someone has felt utterly powerless, it's not surprising that they never want to feel like that again, so instead they move into being

All About Fighting

big and tough. Sometimes fighting feels great. People do it or love watching it because then they can feel powerful when underneath they don't feel powerful at all. So playing a video game where you blow people to bits is often a temporary escape from feeling not at all powerful.'

... the road from pain to violence

Teenagers need to know that experiencing painful loss also can make people exhibit aggressive behaviour. If someone has experienced a painful loss the brain releases aggression chemicals if that loss is not mourned.

Begin the discussion by saying, 'Sometimes loss can make us want to fight. This is because chemicals in the brain which make us aggressive can be activated by the loss, but once you let someone know that you are in pain and let them comfort you the levels of these chemicals go back to normal. At other times, if something bad has happened to you, fighting makes you feel big and strong enough so that nothing that bad will happen again.'

... what trauma is and the effects of trauma

Teenagers who have suffered a shock or trauma have a right to know about how trauma affects people and what can be done about it. They need to know that in post-traumatic stress, the world can feel very hostile for much of the time. People who have suffered trauma live in expectation of further emotional and/or physical attack.

> Re-victimization is actually the central cause of antisocial behaviour.
>
> *(De Mause 2002)*

Of course, history is full of examples of world leaders who were abused as children. They in turn make whole nations suffer because of that abuse.

> The law is anything I write on a piece of paper.
>
> *(Saddam Hussain)*

... how all this can be worsened when life feels too mundane, repetitive and ordinary

Violence can be exciting when life feels too dull.

Specific statements you could use

✸ I can understand that war and fighting can feel really appealing and exciting – either watching it, thinking about doing it or actually doing it. I understand that you can't seem to stop your interest and fascination with it, that you feel compelled to do it as a way of life. But sometimes, it might also feel really exhausting and utterly miserable too.

✸ Perhaps for you, the world feels a too dangerous a place not to fight.

✸ Perhaps the adults in your life hit out with words or with their hands when angry.

✸ When you can't control what happens to you, maybe fighting makes you feel you can have control.

✸ Maybe you've ended up feeling the world is out to get you, because when you were little, it WAS out to get you.

✸ Perhaps you need to feel that you are the one in charge, because if you aren't, it feels too unsafe.

✸ Perhaps you need to be the one with the power, because you never want to go back to the time when you had no power.

✸ Sometimes teenagers fight with their parents because it feels easier to fight them than to admit to themselves that they still need them.

✸ At times, people fight to keep themselves from feeling something they don't want to feel.

All About Fighting

Quotations for Discussion

He was a … child who was very frightened internally. He anticipated attackers and punishments, and he handled this by becoming the attacker.

(Chethik 1989)

I did not invent those horrors; I found them, like everything else, in my memory.

(Jean-Paul Sartre, Words, 1967)

Activities for Development

Museum of Fighting

Divide a large piece of paper into six sections. Ask the teenager to draw in each section a 'museum exhibit' of a time in their life when they wanted to smash, kill or blow things up.

Now ask the teenager to take you around the museum. Help them to address other feelings that they might have been experiencing at the time. You might need to use certain words as prompts, for example, disappointment, let down, hurt, hurting.

Images of War

Show the teenager paintings or drawings of war by famous artists, e.g., Picasso, John Martin, and then ask them to create their own. Now place all the pictures side-by-side.

Ask the teenager which of the professional pictures they like and why and what common features these have with their own picture. Now ask if they have ever felt like the images in one of the professional pictures inside their heads.

Finally, ask them to draw what their life would feel like if they were not fighting anymore.

Vital Psychology for the Practitioner

> When a 6-year-old puts on two six-shooters and a sheriff's badge and struts through the household, he is often attempting to deal with [his] helplessness and smallness.
>
> *(Chethik 1989)*

Common Underlying Causes

✸ Consider if any of the following might fit with what you know of the teenager with whom you are working:

- Harsh childhood where commands, criticisms, nagging, being shouted at, have been the main mode of interaction, and praise or gentle tender interactions have been all too rare.

- Fighting, arguing, and perhaps hitting are common in the family home. Consequently, the teenager's model of relationship is one of fighting rather than gentleness, empathy, tenderness and kindness

- Too many experiences of hopelessness, helplessness, powerlessness.

- Bullied by people at school (staff and/or pupils) and/or people at home (parents and/or siblings)

- Unresolved trauma, e.g., seeing their parents split up or fight.

- Unmourned loss.

- Over-strict parents who the teenager has experienced as having all the power when they have had none.

✸ This is the teenager who is obsessed with images of war, war games and videos, particularly those where you can blow people to pieces. In fact, such teenagers often don't like films without blood and violence, they are just not interested in them.

All About Fighting

✳ Such teenagers often have an overall perception of the world as unsafe. In other words, the teenager doesn't feel safe enough or psychologically secure enough NOT to fight.

- When teenagers have had a life which has dealt them too many painful blows and no one has helped them to work through their feelings, they can find anything to do with war, fighting or violence deeply alluring. This is because in a way the violent film or video game is a mirror for what they feel about the world anyway – that it is basically an unsafe place, a place in which you must protect yourself and be on guard all the time. Furthermore, watching films and playing video games in which you are a potent fighter can make you enjoy, vicariously, a feeling of being the winner, the conqueror, the hero, when in life you may feel quite the opposite.

- When a teenager is defended in this way and presents with a tough look and attitude, they are sometimes not easy to like, as so much of their energy goes into being hard and invulnerable. In so doing all that is good about the human condition: tenderness, warmth, humility, gentleness, seems not to interest them at all and leaves them entirely unmoved.

What brain science tell us about helping teenagers who fight

Teenagers who are securely attached and have not been traumatised tend not to be interested in fighting. Why is this? In secure attachment the brain activates anti-aggression, anti-anxiety chemicals. This means that securely attached teenagers for the most part just don't want to fight. When teenagers have experienced insecure attachment and particularly if there is an overlay of unresolved trauma or loss which has never been properly reflected on or worked through, high levels of stress hormones are repeatedly triggered in the brain. These colour their perception and can make them hyper-alert to any possible threat or danger – so much so that they can see threats even when there aren't any.

It's never too late for teenagers to activate the anti-aggression, anti-anxiety chemicals in their brains. However, for this to happen the chemicals need to be 'awoken', as it were, by a person who the teenager can really trust and believe in and with whom they feel safe enough to be able to open up and relax their defences. This person may well be you!

Fighting in Teenagers who have Suffered Trauma

Recent research (Goodyer 2011) found that in highly traumatised teenagers there was reduced volume in the insular and amygdala. These brain structures are key to the capacity for empathy and the ability to read emotion in others. As yet, we do not know how much they can be repaired. But certainly in terms of prevention, teenagers and children with trauma should be given therapy, ideally very soon after suffering the shock of the trauma. There are many adults with unprocessed trauma and a damaged capacity for empathy which leads them to acts of cruelty and physical or emotional attack on others.

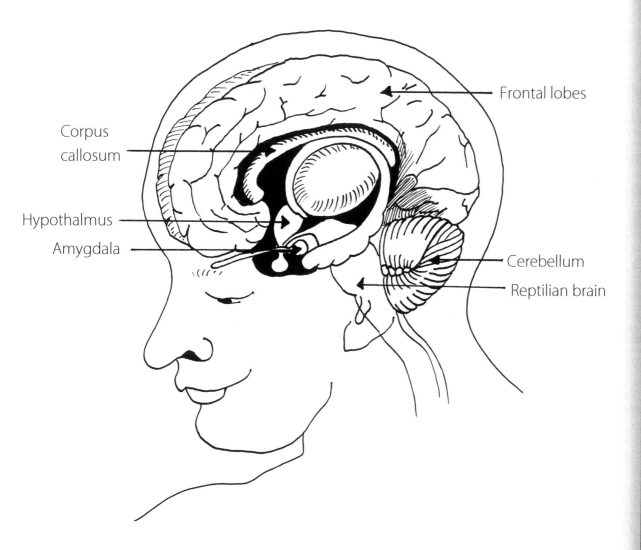

Corpus callosum

Hypothalmus

Amygdala

Frontal lobes

Cerebellum

Reptilian brain

Suffering an Unmourned Major Loss and Fighting

All too frequently in the news we hear about 'love turned to anger'. When we look at the brain chemistry of broken hearts, this is not so surprising.

Pain suffered through loss results in the following:

✳ *A strong activation of the brain chemical 'corticotrophin releasing factor' (CRF) for a sustained period.* This in turn activates the production of high levels of stress hormones (one of which is cortisol) into the brain and body. These can block the release of positive arousal chemicals (including dopamine, opioids and oxytocin). They also activate stress response systems in the brain leading which can lead to depression, anxiety disorders and/or problems with aggression.

✳ *A strong activation of glutamate.* Key to the brain's distress system is a chemical called glutamate. Strong activation of glutamate can dramatically increase crying, whereas blocking glutamate in the brain can dramatically decrease crying. If high levels of glutamate are artificially activated in the brain, the comforting effects of such experiences as music and good company are lost.

✳ *A drop in serotonin.* Low levels of serotonin can increase aggressive impulses, hence some of the angry outbursts of people with broken hearts, jealous feelings or threat of loss. Also, due to the depletion of serotonin, which optimally acts as a mood stabiliser, people are very open to impulsive outbursts of irritation, anger, rage or attacks on the self, resulting in self-harming behaviour.

✳ *Strong activation of acetycholine.* When there is a withdrawal of opioids in the brain, then what are known as 'opponent forces' are released. These opponent forces involve the release of high levels of a chemical called acetycholine. At optimal levels, acetycholine can help us concentrate and feel alert. These high levels of acetycholine can once again make people angry, hostile and attacking.

It is of vital importance that teenagers who have suffered the pain of loss (e.g., parents splitting up, a parent leaving, death of a parent, a parent no longer emotionally available due to own problems) are given comfort over a sustained period.

If a teenager has someone in their life who will comfort their grief, help them reflect on it and work it through, this adverse reaction in brain chemistry, which can set a person on the road to emotional numbing, depression and/or hostility, does not need to happen. The physical process of comforting during grief will release opioids and oxytocin in the brain. These will then block and/or trigger the 'reuptake' of the toxic brain chemicals described above. This is why it is vital for teenagers who are suffering from the pain of loss, rejection and not belonging (even if on the surface they look fine) to receive comfort.

Schools in particular need to be aware of teenagers who have lost a parent or who they think may be 'loving in torment' at home. Many teenagers suffering the pain of loss or rejection behave in very angry or aggressive ways because of their changed brain chemistry. Tragically it is then all too easy for other people to start to hate and punish them and want to exclude them rather than provide help. It must be hoped that increasing knowledge about these dramatic changes in brain chemistry will help to improve levels of compassion in society.

Helping Teenagers to Feel their Sadness

One of the most important life skills is knowing how to suffer well and grieve well. If someone does not have this skill, or if it does not come naturally, then if they are not helped the cost to the self and to others can be very high.

Research shows that sometimes people and animals do actually die of a broken heart (Goodall 1990; Martikainen & Valkonen 1996) Parents who have not been helped to work through the painful losses and separations that they have experienced in their lives may find that their parenting is adversely affected as a result of their grief. Their teenagers may start to develop emotional or behavioural problems. If the parents go into counselling or therapy, their child's problems often stop completely.

Bibliography

Chethik M. (1989) *Techniques of Child Therapy: Psychodynamic Strategies*, The Guilford Press, New York.

De Mause L. (2002) *The Emotional Life of Nations*, Karnac Books, New York.

Goodall J. (1990) *Through a Window: Thirty Years with the Chimpanzees of Gombe*, Weidenfeld & Nicolson, London.

Goodyer I.M. & Fairchild G. (2011) 'Brain structure abnormalities in early-onset and adolescent-onset conduct disorder', *Am J Psychiatry* Jun; Vol. 168(6): 624–33.

Martikainen P. & Valkonen T. (1996) 'Mortality after the death of a spouse: rates and causes of death in a large Finnish cohort', *Am J Public Health*, Aug; Vol. 86(8): 1087–93.

Murray J. (2001) 'TV Violence and Brainmapping in Children', *Psychiatric Times*, XVIII (10).

Post B. (2010) *From Fear to Love*, Post Publishing, Kindle Edition Amazon Media EU.

Bullied, Abused, Used

For teenagers who are angry because they've been bullied, abused or used.

Objective

✷ To enable the teenager to find their 'no'.

✷ To enable teenagers who are perpetrators of abuse to be able to feel again.

✷ To enable teenagers who are perpetrators to talk about how they were abused as children and may still be in the present.

✷ To enable teenagers to understand what is normal in boyfriend-girlfriend relationships and what is abusive.

✷ To heighten the teenager's self-awareness to the point where they are able to appreciate when they are letting themselves be used or abused.

✷ To empower teenagers to find the courage to get the support they need so they no longer remain in abusive situations.

✷ To know the difference between an abusive relationship and a kind warm one.

✷ To know that abuse is never acceptable and a criminal offence.

Bullied, Abused, Used

Guidance for the Worksheet

People often become very unhappy – anxious, angry, depressed or all of these – as a result of being bullied, abused or used in their lives. You may find it useful to think about this in terms of your life, what you want for yourself in the future, and what you might want to change or do differently now.

Have a look at the pictures and the captions. If any of them describe how you feel, please tick the box or colour it in. If none of the pictures describe what you have felt or how you feel now, draw or write in the empty box what it feels like to be bullied or used or abused.

Bullied, Abused, Used

And no-one knows the hell of it, just me

I live in dread of THEM

Hurt or broken

Scared

Dumped on

Used

Like I'm somebody's punch-bag

Wide open to the next attack

Like I've been too bruised by life

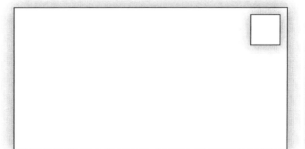

What to Say to the Teenager

Explain what happens in a warm loving caring relationship and what happens in an abusive relationship.

Talk About ...

... why teenagers put up with abusive relationships at home or with partners

Talk about the allure of people, who can be family members or partners, who are loving one minute and abusive the next and how this can set up an addiction. After all, an abusive person is not usually abusive all of the time. There is a temptation to just put up with the painful bits of the relationship, and wait for the return of the loving bits. Explain to the teenager that if their parent or carer was emotionally responsive some of the time and not at others when they were younger, this can make them particularly vulnerable to putting up with abusive teenage partners.

Try to help the teenagers to understand that if a person has a childhood where they suffered the pain of unmet needs for love, warmth, safety and security, such needs don't just go away. The natural human response in the teenage years is to feel (often totally outside of conscious awareness) now my boyfriend/girlfriend will make up for everything I didn't get in my childhood. So the teenager will go into relationship desperate to be loved and needed unconditionally.

They need to know that the way to stop themselves being so vulnerable to repeatedly suffering heartache in relationships is to talk about the pain of their childhood and to address the emptiness inside their desperate need to be loved. They need to hear this in a way that does not attack their parents, but rather for it to be explained that parents often cannot love in the way they would like to, due to their own problems caused by a lack of unconditional love in their own childhood.

Explain how it is common when in an abusive relationship where you love someone to just play down the abuse to yourself.

... the fear that standing up to the abuser will result in more abuse

The teenagers need to know that this is very common, but that in the UK there are a great many protective agencies to ensure that this won't happen and where relevant, as abuse is a criminal offence, the police can be involved and stop things once and for all.

... what shame is, what it feels like and what can be done about it

Shame works by attacking not simply one aspect of someone, such as a skill, an act or behaviour, but their personhood – their very *being*. Shame derails thinking, functioning, decision-making and self-worth, because it is an assault on the self, a real shock to the system.

A shaming experience in the playground can give someone the feeling of being flawed for years afterwards.

Teenagers will often pick up on any difference as a target for teasing, bullying or shaming. The difference might be having the 'wrong' accent, size, shape, colour, clothes, trainers, or a vulnerability such as dyslexia or a speech impediment. If the teenager is already shy or anxious and has low self-worth, this can confirm their feelings of being not all right in some fundamental way.

If someone has been badly shamed, it can put them off wanting to approach people for potential new friendships. They may become defensive and fearful instead.

As Casement (1985) states, 'Part of the problem was that her emotional scars were not visible.'

Teenagers can stop suffering from the effects of being shamed if someone will listen and empathise with the pain they have suffered, and can help them with it - as was not done when they originally experienced the feeling of shame.

Bullied, Abused, Used

Sources of Help for Teenagers in the UK

An excellent Home Office issued leaflet for teenagers
www.homeoffice.gov.uk/publications/crime/teen-relationship-abuse/teen-abuse-leaflet?view=Binary

ChildLine
0800 1111
www.childline.org.uk
Free confidential helpline for children and young people.

Get Connected
0808 808 4994
www.getconnected.org.uk
Free confidential helpline for young people aged under 25.

The Hideout
www.thehideout.org.uk
A website which helps children and teenagers to understand domestic abuse and what to do.

NSPCC
0808 800 5000
www.nspcc.org.uk
Free confidential helpline for children and young people.

Rape Crisis
0800 808 9999
www.rapecrisis.org.uk
Helpline and information about rape and sexual abuse and what you can do.

Respect Not Fear
www.respectnotfear.co.uk
Information about abusive relationships and what to do.

Respect 4 Us
www.respect4us.org.uk

Quotations for Discussion

'Everyone has been overlooked at times, forgotten, slighted, rejected and unheard, unseen, uninvited, unwelcomed, short-changed, and unfairly dealt with. Since the deep roots of hurt often remain unseen by those who bear its heavy burden, they treat their pain like an illegitimate child, having no proper parentage or position.'

(Bar-Levav 1988)

'When individuals, families and groups of people are emotionally damaged they can't help hurting themselves or those around them. In trying to rid themselves of their own pain they unwittingly damage others.'

(Orbach 1994)

This Be the Verse
They fuck you up, your mum and dad.
They may not mean to, but they do.
They fill you with the faults they had
And add some extra, just for you.

(Philip Larkin, 1971)

Activities for Development

Useful exercises for development are the worksheets 'Encouragers and Rubbishers' (see page 175), and 'My Relationships Past and Present' (see page 162).

Vital Psychology for the Practitioner

Common Underlying Causes

Consider if any of the following might fit with what you know of the teenager with whom you are working:

✳ Bullied at home

✳ Bullied at school

✳ Sibling abuse (a more common occurrence than parental abuse)

✳ Verbal abuse/physical abuse/sexual abuse

✳ Abusive boyfriend/girlfriend relationships

Victims of Current Abuse

If a teenager is suffering from bullying or abuse, this needs to be taken very seriously because there is a strong link between being bulled and teenage suicide. A 2010 report by Beatbullying (based on figures from the Office of National Statistics) found that bullying at school is to blame for almost half of the UK's teenage suicides: 75 percent of those suicides were by hanging, only 6 percent took pills. There was a higher tendency to suicide in girls than boys.

Case Study – Bullying Leading to Suicide

Phoebe Prince, 15, moved from Ireland to the United States. She hanged herself after girls at her new school used internet chat rooms to bully her, calling her an 'Irish slut' and other hurtful insults.

Sam was bullied at school in Gloucestershire, and via the social networking site Bebo. The taunts finally drove the quiet, music-loving teenager to hang himself in his bedroom.

(News of the World, *June 2010*)

Being bullied interferes with every aspect of life. It can destroy self-esteem, confidence, joy in life, spontaneity and curiosity. It often dramatically undermines academic achievement as it can derail clear thinking, attention and concentration. It can interfere with any enjoyment of calm in terms of blocking the brain's natural anti-anxiety chemicals. Being bullied can also result in a teenager losing faith in the value of human relationships. Instead, they commonly withdraw from relating to others in any meaningful way and take refuge in the Internet and turn to cyber-relationships in social chat rooms rather than real relationships. Suicide is an extreme version social withdrawal – the pull to withdraw from life completely.

If the teenager talks about bullying at home, consider also whether there is bullying at school and vice versa. Just because the teenager talks of bullying at school, do not assume there will be no bullying at home too, this could be from either a sibling or parent. Some parents tend to play down sibling abuse – but frequently being called names and put-down by a sibling constitutes bullying. Thirdly also ask about boyfriend-girlfriends relationships. If there is violence or abuse at home, teenagers are vulnerable to either being abusive or being a victim of abuse in their intimate relationships.

Abusive Boyfriend-Girlfriend Relationships

Society is very focused on child abuse and so abuse of teenagers by other teenagers, an extremely common occurrence particularly in sexual relationships, often gets far too little attention. As Barter (2009) rightly says, 'This may be due to professional perceptions about the heightened vulnerability of younger children, or the view that adolescents may be more able to protect themselves from abuse.' When a teenager is being abused by a partner we should also should not underestimate the emotional impact that this has on their peers, especially when the teenager remains in an abusive relationship.

Abuse from a Parent

'His forehead had made violent contact with the door handle and he had screamed out in pain. Then he had seen his father's expression, the one that warned him of the dangers of screaming out loud, the expression which instructed him always to scream inwardly and never again to let anyone know that he had been hurt.'

(Cook 1991)

Again, teenagers need to know and understand what is normal behaviour and what is abusive.

Bibliography

Bar-Levav R. (1988) *Thinking in the Shadow of Feelings*, Simon & Schuster, New York.

Barter C. (2009) 'In the Name of Love: Exploitation and Violence in Teenage Dating Relationships', *British Journal of Social Work*, Vol. 39: 211–233.

Casement P. (1985) *On Learning From the Patient*, Routledge, London.

Cook D. (1991) *Second Best*, Faber & Faber, London.

Larkin P. (1990) *Collected Poems*, Faber & Faber, London.

Orbach S. (1994) *What's Really Going On Here?*, Virago, London.

Bullied, Abused, Used

Like a Nightmare Got Stuck in my Brain

For teenagers who are angry because they've experienced trauma or traumatic loss.

Objective

✸ To understand what shock is and how it can affect the mind and body over time.

✸ To understand how traumatic stress gets into your body and needs releasing.

✸ To be able to talk about and feel 'the time the bad thing happened' and feel really listened to and understood.

✸ To help the teenager to work through their trauma or traumatic loss to the point of resolution.

✸ To validate the teenager's anger about the shock and help them to access their other more vulnerable feelings about it such as hurt, fear, impotence and grief.

Like a Nightmare Got Stuck in my Brain

Guidance for the Worksheet

It is easy to think that your life will always carry on down the same path, with roughly the same people and in roughly the same way. Then one day something happens that changes everything. Often, the change involves some form of loss: loss of a loved one; loss of a place like your school; loss of something safe and known in your life; loss of self-respect; loss of the respect of others; loss of a feeling of safety in being in the world. Whatever it is, things are literally never the same again.

Terrible shocks are something the vast majority of us will have to manage at some time during our lives. Without help to talk about these shocks however, some people can suffer from long-term psychological problems. Sometimes the shock gets locked in the body as well as the mind, resulting in illness and/or physical symptoms. Being in a state of shock can also affect the ability to concentrate at school.

This exercise will help you to think about the shocks you have experienced, and to find words for your feelings, so that the memories of the shock lose their power.

Look at the pictures and think of a shock or shocks you have suffered in your life. Did any of them make you feel like any of the pictures? If so, tick or colour in the appropriate picture. If not, draw your own images in the empty box and give your picture a title.

✷ What was the worst thing for you about the shock?

✷ What words could you use to describe it?

✷ How do you think the shock still affects you?

Like a Nightmare Got Stuck in my Brain

When the bad thing happened it felt like …

A door slammed in my face.

Everything falling out of everything.

A punch in my gut.

A great smash.

A terrible noise.

Everything coming to a standstill.

The world coming to an end.

Talk About ...

... common causes of shock particular to the teenage years

(See below in the section on psychology.)

... what post-traumatic shock is and its symptoms

(See below in the section on psychology.)

... the anger or cruelty that can result after a teenager has been traumatised

(See below in the section on psychology.)

... trauma resulting from the teenager making a bad decision and the vital role of parental response

If the shock is a result of something the teenager had done in an impulsive moment without thinking (e.g., getting in trouble with the police, becoming pregnant or getting someone pregnant) a key issue is whether the teenager's parents, under these circumstances, are 'lie invitees' or 'truth tellers'.

This is a very useful distinction devised by the therapist Ellyn Bader, and concerns how easy or difficult it is for teenagers to discuss sensitive issues with attachment figures.

If teenagers try to discuss their bad decisions with parents, and the latter fly off the handle, the parents are 'lie invitees'. This means that these teenagers are likely to start lying to their parents because telling the truth leaves them emotionally dsyregulated, feeling shamed, guilty and generally worse off. When parents are 'lie invitees', teenagers can be left battling alone with traumatic distress resulting from their ill thought-out actions for years. It may not occur to them to go to a counsellor or another adult for help.

If the parents are 'truth tellers' the teenager is fortunate indeed, because even when they mess up (as teenagers inevitably do) their parents listen and are focused on finding the best way forward.

... the pain from suddenly being dumped by a girlfriend/boyfriend

Teenagers need to know that, sadly, partner relationships in the teenage years are often an experience of going from being very, very happy to being very, very hurt. This can be a real shock. They need to understand that it is impossible to reach adulthood without having been deeply hurt on many occasions. The important thing is how you deal with it. Some people, for example, deal with it by using drink or drugs, but very many who do this suffer early an death.

More than two thousand years ago Virgil knew that hurt was to be found everywhere, 'Had I a hundred tongues, a hundred lips, a throat of iron and a chest of brass, I could not tell Man's countless suffering.' (Virgil, *Aeneid*)

Hurt is so painful that we often choose to deny or repress it instead of facing up to it.

The teenager needs to know that the best way of soothing pain is to talk about it with an empathic adult.

Quotations for Discussion

When my house burnt down I could see the rising sun.

(Anon.)

In traumatic stress we become frightened unthinking animals.

(Van der Kolk 2003)

The hushed network of nightmare. You have lost touch with the sustaining ordinariness of things.

(Fanthorpe 1996)

This is me, this is my life and this is going to be my future. But, sometimes we get it wrong – and in comes a big shock.

(Dorothy Rowe, 2003)

But our minds were still out of breath…

(Siegfried Sassoon, 1996)

When young lips have drunk deep of the bitter waters of Hate, Suspicion and Despair, all the Love in the world will not take away that knowledge.

(Rudyard Kipling, Baa Baa Black Sheep, 1888)

Activities for Development

Shock Energies

Using a large piece of paper, ask the teenager to think about one shock in particular. Ask them to draw the energetic charge they feel when they think of that particular shock.

Alternatively, if you have access to musical instruments, ask the teenager to play out the energy of the shock. As shock can leave a teenager feeling helpless or impotent, it can also be very healing to take the power back, through drama, drums or voice, in terms of making an energised protest in this way.

Vital Psychology for the Practitioner

Common Underlying Causes

Consider if any of the following fit with what you know of the teenager with whom you are working:

* Has suffered a traumatic loss

* Has been suddenly dumped by a girlfriend or boyfriend

* Parents are separating/divorcing/fighting

* A parent has left

* A pet has died

* A parent has become ill or died

* Has changed of schools

* They have made a bad decision and become involved with the police

* They have taken drugs which have messed up their minds

* They are pregnant or have made someone pregnant

> 750,000 children witness domestic violence each year, overall 30 per cent of girls and 16 per cent of boys have experienced some form of family violence.
>
> *(Home Office Statistics 2010)*

Often teenagers just feel generally awful (depressed, angry, anxious) and don't realise they are in shock or indeed what shock does to the body. For some teenagers using this worksheet may be the first time that they have acknowledged to themselves the power of the shock, so that it can be properly worked through. Without this vital trauma-processing work, to quote Henry Maudsely, 'The sorrow that hath no vent in tears makes other organs weep'. It may help to talk to teenagers, when appropriate, about the cost to emotional health of bottling up feelings about shock.

Consider Post-Traumatic Stress

If the teenager suffers from persistent states of one or more of the following: hyper-arousal, hyper-vigilance, flashbacks, startle reactions, generalised anxiety, agitation, angry outbursts, flashbacks, social phobias, nightmares, problems concentrating at school, anxiety attacks, depression, inappropriate flight/freeze responses (suddenly finding their thinking, feeling or doing is frozen or blocked), feeling that the shock happened only yesterday, then they are probably suffering from post-traumatic stress disorder (PTSD).

In post-traumatic stress, core arousal and stress response systems in the brain can be highly affected. This means the body is unable to regulate its internal systems properly, resulting in physical symptoms such as problems with sleeping, eating, breathing, digestion, and elimination. Ask the teenager if they are suffering from any of these and then if the answer is positive, you may need to refer on as appropriate. Consider making a referral to a family doctor, or CAMHS (Children & Adolescent Mental Health Service) or child psychotherapist.

When a Shock is Locked in the Body

It is best to enable teenagers to feel so safe with you that, as a result of talking about their trauma, they naturally move into releasing the shock from their body in the form of howling, crying, shaking and shouting.

If this happens it is vital that you do not get frightened, overwhelmed or thrown by the intensity of the discharge (it is simply part of the human condition). If you feel you might be overwhelmed, don't embark on this with the teenager, stay more in the thinking reflective brain and then refer on to someone who is comfortable with such a release.

If the high levels of bodily arousal are not released, the teenager can remain in PTSD.

> 'When the reptilian brain perceives danger, it activates an extraordinary amount of energy … designed to give the [person] every advantage it needs to defend itself. The catch is that to avoid being traumatized, the [person] must use up all the energy that has been mobilized to deal with the threat. Whatever energy is not discharged does not simply go away; instead, it lingers, creating the potential for traumatic reaction to occur…. In short, an untraumatized outcome to a threatening situation depends on one's ability to remain engaged in action, … and to discharge the energy that has been mobilized, thereby allowing the nervous system to return to its accustomed level of functioning.'
>
> *(Levine 2006)*

Working Anger Resulting from Trauma

If anger is exhibited as a result of trauma, it is necessary to reach the victim behind the aggressor and understand the hurt as well as the anger. If we don't teenagers can be vulnerable to act out on others what has been done to them – but this time with someone else as a victim. In short, 're-victimization' is a very common result of trauma if the teenager has not worked through their feelings about the shock.

Teenagers need to know that there is a part of the brain called the amygdala that stores traumatic memories. When they over-react with anger to something other people take in their stride, they need to know that often this is because the amygdala has been triggered which causes a cascade of stress hormones to wash over the brain resulting in primitive states of flight or fight.

The really annoying thing about the amygdala is that the brain doesn't tell you that you are remembering something horrible from your past. So you think that it is just what is happening in the present that is making you feel this way. But there is a clue. If someone reacts with over-the-top intensity to a situation, or to something that others take in their stride, it is likely that a traumatic memory has been triggered. It will be helpful to show them where the amgydala is in the brain. (See Brain Illustration, page 135).

Cruelty Resulting from Trauma

> The trauma keeps them rigidly fixated on the past, making them fight the last battle over and over again.
>
> *(van der Kolk 1996)*

> Trauma demands repetition.
>
> *(Selma Fraiberg 1987)*

Teenagers who have been traumatised may find themselves being cruel to others. It can help to explain to them how the mind works in trauma and explain that re-victimization (making others feel what we feel) is not uncommon.

Case Study – Tommy (age 16)

Tommy presented as angry and tough all the time. He was a bully and enjoyed the power he felt from it. No one messed with Tommy.

When he was three years old, Tommy saw his dad beat up his mum and he couldn't do anything about it, but just sit and watch. He probably took a decision then (outside of his conscious awareness) never to let himself feel impotent again. When the counsellor empathised with the terrified, desperately alone little boy underneath, Tommy started to feel again and over time became charming, approachable and academically very successful.

Bibliography

Fanthorpe U.A. (1996) 'Walking in Darkness', pp. 51–55 in Dunn S., Morrison B. & Roberts M. (eds), *Mind Readings – Writers' Journeys Through Mental States*, London: Minerva.

Fraiberg S. (1987) *Selected Writings of Selma Fraiberg*, ed. Louis Fraiburg, Ohio State University Press.

Home Office (2010) 'Expect Respect: A Toolkit for addressing Teenage Relationship', http://thisisabuse.direct.gov.uk

Kipling R. (1995) *Baa Baa, Black Sheep*, Penguin, Harmondsworth.

Levine P. (2006) *Trauma Through a Child's Eyes: Awakening the Ordinary Miracle of Healing*, North Atlantic Books.

Rowe D. (2003) *Depression: The Way Out of the Prison*, Routledge, London.

Sassoon S. (1996) in *Traumatic Stress: The Effects of Overwhelming Experience on Mind, Body and Society*, van der Kolk B.A., McFarlane C.A. & Weiseth L., The Guildford Press, New York.

Van der Kolk B.A., McFarlane C.A. & Weiseth, L. (1996) *Traumatic Stress: The Effects of Overwhelming Experience on Mind, Body and Society*, The Guildford Press, New York.

My Relationships Past & Present

For teenagers who are angry and/or suffer as a result of another's anger, because they have experienced too many relationships that have been based on power and control.

Objective

To help teenagers to take a step back from their relationships (past and present), and review and understand which are on the whole supportive, empowering and kind and which are about having 'power over' and control.

My Relationships Past & Present

Guidance for the Worksheet

It is all too easy for people to find themselves playing victim or dominator roles or in other words 'power-over' and 'power-under' roles in their important relationships. 'Power-over' or dominant interactions can be found, for example, in nagging, controlling, criticising, put-downs. In contrast, when someone adopts a power-under or submissive position, this can lead to feelings of impotence, low self-esteem and general misery.

This exercise aims to help you to become more aware of submission/dominance patterns in your relationships (both past and present). From this place of awareness you might want to make some changes in your life and in your relationships.

✳ Look at the drawings of 'power-over' patterns of relating and the drawings of co-operative relationships, known as 'power-with'.

✳ Write 'Me' next to the figures that best represent you in some of the key relationships in your life past or present.

✳ Now write the names of the other people in your life next to the figures which best represent them. Try to be as honest with yourself as you can.

✳ Draw more scenes in the empty boxes if you need them.

✳ Now stand back and look at what you have written or drawn. What have you learned?

✳ Are you more often the dominant one in a relationship, the submissive one, or a mixture of both?

✳ Maybe you have played different roles in different relationships in your life? Perhaps the roles in relationships in your childhood are different from the roles you play today.

✳ Do you have any of the co-operative relationships in your life too?

✳ If, in your relationships today you are still finding yourself in too many 'power-over' or 'power-under' interactions, what can you do to change things?

✳ How might you be with people and/or choose the people you are with to ensure that for more of the time you enjoy 'power-with' interactions?

✳ If you repeatedly find yourself being submissive or dominant in your relationships, think about what you might be playing out from painful relationships in your past. We tend to repeat painful relationship patterns from the past as either victim or persecutor. For example, if you had strict dominant parents who always needed to be in charge are you being like that now in your relationships? Or are you being the opposite? As you had to submit to that dominant parent are you still being too submissive in your current relationships, as if you were with your dad all over again?

You may find it useful to think about these issues in terms of your overall life and relationships and what you want for the rest of your life, the things you might want to change or do differently.

My Relationships Past & Present

My Relationships Past & Present

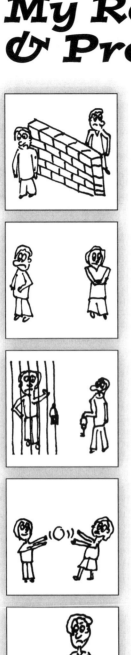

What to Say to the Teenager

What you say depends on the direction the conversation takes in relation to the pictures. If it is clear that the teenager has experience of being the victim in power-over relationships, and the discussion becomes more specific regarding abuse, you might find some of the statistics shown below useful (see 'Vital Psychology for the Practitioner'). For example, someone who been disciplined in harsh ways who now finds himself hitting his girlfriend may find the statistics on physical abuse very sobering.

In addition, the statements about abusing or being abused in the following section may be a useful part of your follow-on discussion about power and control.

Some teenagers need psycho-education about what is abusive and what is not. If a high level of anger has been the culture in the childhood home, they may view as acceptable in their teenage partner relationships behaviours that are actually abusive. Many statements from the 'Vital Psychology' section can help with this confusion.

Discussion can focus on the stark contrast of the warm, kind, gentle, tender relationship and the one that is brutal, harsh, angry and all about power.

It is worth remembering that cyberbullying and sexual coercion can be key to power issues in teenage relationships.

Talk About ...

... the brain science on bullying

It may be appropriate to inform the teenager that we now know that bullying damages the brain and particularly the social/emotionally intelligent brain (Teicher et al 2010). The jury remains out in terms of whether the damage can be repaired.

... why some teenagers are vulnerable in terms of staying in abusive relationships

You could begin the discussion by saying something like:
'When teenagers have not felt very loved and valued in childhood, they can be particularly vulnerable to putting up with abuse in partner relationships if their partner shows them love *some of the time* or even *just a bit* of the time. This means they often stay in very emotionally poor relationships and put up with all sorts of unkindness or cruelty that other teenagers wouldn't dream of putting up with. It is a question of "seeing rarities as pearls".

And then, when you have taken far too much hurtful behaviour – emotional and/or physical – you can get a text saying something like "You are so dumped!" If the partner is cruel in the relationship they are unlikely to be any different in the way they end it.'

Comments posted by teenagers on the internet:

I just want someone who'll never give me up, let me down, run around, or hurt me.

(DirectGov 2011)

I loved him with all my heart but he just took away every drop of hope I had, he crushed my heart. Don't trust a boy wit your life coz he will just abuse that.

(thisisabuse.direct.gov.uk 2011)

... why some teenagers put up with abuse, cruelty or emotional neglect in their relationship with a partner

Research has shown that the majority of girls who experience abuse remained in the relationships for a considerable time. Generally, as the relationship progressed so did the levels of violence and the fear (Sugarman & Hotaling 1989). Most had also experienced abusive relationships in childhood.

Very many teenagers who put up with abuse do so because they are trying to make up for a 'love made hungry' from childhood. This means they go into intimate teenager relationship too emotionally hungry for love, because they never felt really loved as a child.

Many children pick up all too easily that they are found to be irritating, annoying and too life-restricting to their parents. So they try (quite unconsciously) to get all the love from their teenage relationships that they didn't get as small children. In this quest, they will put up with far too much in the relationship – name-calling, coercive control (see following section) and sometimes even being hit.

By contrast, teenagers who have been loved and who are emotionally secure with good self-esteem, know what a loving tender relationship feels like, what happens, what is said and done. So when they encounter abuse they tend to end that relationship very quickly.

Research shows that when teenagers have dreams and career aspirations, they are also not as vulnerable to abuse. However, if their boyfriend or girlfriend is the teenager's only source of self-esteem they will put up with all sorts of violence. So these 'alternative sources of self-esteem' (Barter 2009) offer a protective factor against staying in relationships with violent, abusive, controlling partners. Research has shown that the girls with aspirations felt that 'their education was more important than having a serious boyfriend' (DirectGov 2011).

Activities for Development

Power Replays

Ask the teenager to think about their 'early training' during childhood in terms of submission/dominance modes of relating.

Using sandplay miniatures, drawing or clay, ask the teenager to depict relationships in their childhood or adolescence when they were in a submissive position and an adult in their life (e.g., a teacher, parent, bully or other relative) was adopting a 'power-over' way of relating.

Ask the teenager to write down what they would want to say to those people who abused power in this way. Finally, ask them to look at how, sub-consciously, they might be replaying 'power-over' ways of relating in their lives now, either as a victim or persecutor.

You might like to explain to the teenager the psychoanalytic term 'identification with the aggressor'. This means that, despite our best intentions, we can treat another person in the negative ways we were treated. In other words, we bully as we have been bullied and control as we have been controlled. It is often only as a result of working through our feelings about the original 'persecutor', and the shame, fear and humiliation that we can stop doing this.

Vital Psychology for the Practitioner

> In the UK around a third of boys and a quarter of girls admit to having bullied other children.
>
> *(Katz et al 2001)*

Common Underlying Causes

Consider if any of the following might fit with what you know of the teenager with whom you are working:

✳ Over-strict parents

✳ Teenagers who've been disciplined in harsh ways

✳ Insecurely attached teenagers

✳ Teenagers whose parents have too often modelled relationships as being about power and control

✳ Teenagers who are bullies or who have been bullied

✳ Teenagers who adopt the persona of persecutor or victim in teenager partner relationships

Physical Abuse in Teenage Relationships

> • 1 in 4 teenage girls have been hit by a boyfriend
> • 1 in 9 report severe physical abuse
> • 72 percent of girls and 51 percent of boys reported some form of emotional partner violence.
> • 13-year-old girls were as likely to report physical violence in their intimate relationships as those aged 16.
>
> *(Home Office 2010)*

Girls report that physical attacks often occur not as a result of an argument but rather as a means of establishing dominance. Many teenage girls attempt to justify the abuse by saying that the boy just can't control his feelings of love and jealousy or felt is was just a kind of uncontrolled caring.

Teenagers Talking

He bit me on the face, it was horrible, really disgusting. Because when I was trying to show my point of view, he doesn't appreciate it.

'I caught her snogging another boy. So I slapped her and beat him up.'
'And how did you feel afterwards, when you did hit her and beat him up?'
'I was upset, about that she could do that to me...I had to though, 'cos...' '
What do you think about it now when you look back on it?'
'Um, I think I was right to do it.'

(Barter et al 2009)

Emotional Abuse & coercive control

59 per cent of girls and 50 per cent of boys reported instigating emotional abuse.

(Barter et al 2009)

Emotional abuse in teenage partner relationships often entails verbal abuse:

✳ Calling their partner names

✳ Put-downs about their partner's body, appearance, family members or friends

✳ Making fun of their partner

✳ Making the girl's sexual history public with their mates

✳ Transacting through orders and commands

✳ Threatening to hurt partners unless they do what they want

✳ Telling partners who they can and cannot see

✳ Telling partners where they can and cannot go

✳ Constantly checking up on what partners are doing by phone or text (SMS)

✳ Using their friends to keep their partners under observation

✳ Isolating partners from friends or family

In effect, this results in reducing the teenager to being a dependent child again. Often teenagers stay in these relationships even though all the control made them very unhappy.

Teenagers Talking

He tells me I'm fat all the time, even though I'm size 10. He tells me I'm nothing without him and he's doing me a favour by being with me and he could do better … He gets paranoid if I go out with my mates on a Saturday night, thinking I'm cheating on him and reads my texts. Whereas, I'm not allowed to know what he's up to ever, even just out of curiosity.

(Direct Gov 2010)

You must not go out in those clothes – only in these clothes. You must have no contact with that person anymore. Like when I'd be out with my friends and he'd drag me off and say he didn't want me out any longer and I'd got to go in and it could be like half past six. I'd say they're my friends I'll speak to whoever I want to and then he'd get really mad. If I did see the people he didn't want you to see … he'd physically drag me away from them.

(Barter et al 2009)

Sexual Abuse in Teenage Relationships

31 per cent of girls and 16 per cent of boys reported some form of sexual partner violence. About half of the boys interviewed said that the main reason they were in the relationship was for sex and in some cases it was the only reason.

(Barter et al 2009)

It does seem that many boys are interested in the physical rather than emotional aspects of intimate relationships. Sexual abuse in teenage relationships means pressure or physically forcing the teenage partner into kissing, touching or sex. There can be threats to end the relationship if the person doesn't comply, or telling other people how frigid they are. Many boys describe this as 'just messing around'.

Teenagers Talking

He tried to make me have sex with him … and first of all I was like 'no, no, no … because I hadn't done it before, he was like 'go on, go on, go on' and I was like 'no' and then I finally like give in to him and we went off to go and do it. Oh my god, and he made me suck his dick and it was horrible …

See with my relationship it wasn't up to me … [when to have sex]

Afterwards … I just couldn't, I couldn't even look at myself in the mirror … but the weirdest thing is you still go back, we still go back to them, because we have feelings for them obviously, but we shouldn't have went back to them.

I only went out with him for a week. And then … 'cos I didn't want to do what he wanted to do [sex] he just started … hitting me.

To say 'no' is really kind of big … so when he was trying to force me I just went with the flow really. I was just crying, I was just crying and crying and crying.

… I can't believe I done it … I regret it so badly, that's the most horrible most stupid thing I've done in my whole life.

He was saying stuff like 'Oh yeah, she was proper horrible', [nervous laughing] that I couldn't do it and I was like 'Well, I've never done it before'.

So obviously with a loose girl you would talk to her different, you would treat her different because you would know that you would get something easier. But a decent girl you would treat her with more respect, innit? And try and be like, you wouldn't say certain things to her. Because you know she is decent.

(Barter et al 2009)

Cyberbullying

Cyberbullying is the use of mobile phones or the Internet to humiliate or threaten partners or other teenagers. In research on text message (SMS) and cyber-bullying undertaken by Smith et al (2008) it was shown that nearly half of the girls and a third of the boys reported this.

Perpetrators of abuse

If we just write bullies off as bad, we don't need to reflect on their childhood experiences in which there has clearly been a gross failure of empathy at some level. For teenagers not to be distress averse (feeling pain at the pain of others), somewhere along the line they cut off from their own pain. People only do this when there is a lack of emotional responsiveness from the adults who take care of them.

These teenagers need to be helped to feel again. This will only happen if they are themselves on the receiving end of empathic listening, particularly in relation to their emotional pain in infancy or childhood.

How to recognise common symptoms of abuse

Some of the following may be indicative of abuse in teenagers:

✹ Schoolwork going down-hill

✹ Problems with anxiety, depression, irritation

✹ Developing neurotic symptoms (e.g., checking rituals)

✹ Physical injuries which are passed off as 'accidents'

✹ Distancing from friends or family

✹ Abuse of drugs or alcohol

✹ Cancelling of social engagements

Bibliography

Barter C. (2009) 'Safeguarding young people from exploitation and violence in teenage 'dating' relationships', Research Project, University of Bristol.

Barter C., McCarry M., Berridge D. & Evans K. (2009) *Partner exploitation and violence in teenage intimate relationships*, NSPCC & University of Bristol, nspcc.org.uk.

DirectGov (2011) www.thisisabuse.direct.gov.uk

Katz A., Buchanan A. & Bream V. (2001) *Bullying in Britain: testimonies from Teenagers*, Young Voice, East Molesey.

Smith P.K., Mahdavi J., Carvalho M., Fisher S., Russell, S. & Tippett, N. (2008) 'Cyberbullying: its nature and impact in secondary school pupils', *Journal of Child Psychology & Psychiatry*, Vol. 49: 376–85.

Sugarman D.B. & Hotaling G.T. (1989) 'Dating violence: Prevalence, context, and risk markers', in Pirog-Good A.A. & Stets J.E. (eds) *Violence in dating relationships: Emerging social issues*, Praeger, New York.

Teicher M.H., Samson J.A., Sheu Y.S., Polcari A. & McGreenery C.E. (2010) 'Hurtful words: association of exposure to peer verbal abuse with elevated psychiatric symptom scores and corpus callosum abnormalities', *Am J Psychiatry*, Dec; Vol. 167(12): 1464–71.

My Relationships Past & Present

The Encouragers &
The Rubbishers

For teenagers who are angry because they've experienced too much shame and discouragement.

> We may choose to grow, to stagnate or to decline and in a world where there is little encouragement to grow, most of us may not do it very much or at all.
>
> *(Rowan 1986)*

Objective

✷ To enable teenagers to become more aware of the impact of people in their lives who have encouraged them and those who have criticised them, put them down, made them feel not good enough or even feel like rubbish. Having this awareness may lead to them taking action about who they spend time with.

✷ To become more aware of how the internalising of negative or discouraging messages contribute to self-sabotage and a feeling of not being good enough, so that dreams are not realised and ambitions not fulfilled. If not named and brought into consciousness these internalised negative messages may continue to undermine the fulfilment of potential in the teenager's life.

✷ To help the teenagers establish self-worth on their own terms separate from the discouragements or put downs they have received from others.

✷ To enable the teenager to feel believed in by you.

✷ To help the teenagers find value in themselves.

✷ To enable the teenager to appreciate that they do not have to remain passive in their response to shaming and discouragement.

✷ To empower teenagers to find a healthy (and not destructive) anger and means of protest in response to the blight of put down.

The Encouragers & The Rubbishers

Guidance for the Worksheet

Some people criticise and discourage. Others encourage, praise and support.

Discouragement can have a lethal effect on what you feel about yourself and any dreams you might have. It can squash your dreams, leaving you with little belief in yourself or your abilities.

On the other hand, encouragement can give you the vital energy to go after what you want in life and to be successful. You may find it useful to think about this in terms of your whole life and what you want for the rest of your life, what you might want to change or do differently.

It might also be helpful to think about this using some pictures. Have a look at the pictures on the worksheet.

Write above the pictures of the stars, the sun and the trophy the names of any people in your life who have encouraged you or really valued something about you. Your relationship with these people has made you feel better about yourself.

Above the rain, thunder clouds, mess and crushing boot write the names of people in your life who have discouraged you, brought you down and made you feel bad about yourself.

The Encouragers & The Rubbishers

Encouragers

Rubbishers

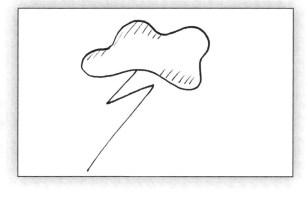

What to Say to the Teenager

Help the Teenager Access their Anger

Discuss the following quotation and hep the teenager to access their anger about the discouragements and put-downs they have experienced.

> Anger helps us reassert our sense of power and maintain our dignity and self-respect.
>
> *(Bar Levav 1988)*

Avoid Reassurances

It is a well-known saying that 'Reassurances never reassured anyone'. Certainly not a sceptical, cynical teenager.

'But *I* like you', you may feel tempted to say to the teenager who sees themselves as rubbish. However, for many teenagers who have been very discouraged in life, if you do say this they will think, 'This praise does not fit with the person I know I am inside.'

As Brian Keenan (1992) noted, 'If you put a diamond collar on a dog, it's still a dog made more ludicrous by the diamonds around its neck.' It is better to empathise with how painful it must be to feel unworthy, unlovable and not good at anything and to emphasise that the adults in their lives have not done a good job at clearly and frequently voicing appreciation.

Talk About ...

> Most importantly we know that positive self-regard can only be attained relationally.
>
> *(Sunderland 2003)*

... hypnotic-induction

Hypnotic induction is the internalising of negative messages, whether verbal or non-verbal, particularly from early childhood. Such messages tend to be swallowed whole, believed fully and then played in the mind repeatedly as if they were the child's own views – while he or she has forgotten who said them or implied them in the first place.

Often, it's not that a parent or teacher has actually said anything discouraging but instead that the teenager has just picked up that for a lot of the time they are experienced as irritating, annoying and wearisome.

Help teenagers to become more aware of the negative things they say to themselves in their heads – the daily messages which can be both energy-draining and confidence-sapping. Ask the teenagers to talk about what these messages are and who they think might have said them in the first place. By bringing these messages and self-criticisms more into awareness teenagers can gain more power over them and have more choice as to whether or not they should go on playing them in their heads.

... the power of encouragement

If the teenager has said that no one ever encourages them, ask if anyone ever did so in their childhood. They may have known someone at that time who really believed in them and from whom they can still draw strength and comfort in their mind, even if they no longer see the person in reality. Talking about this special person – and sharing memories about them with you – is an important 'bringing to life' of that person and their potent positive messages.

Explain that encouragement usually comes from those who have the generosity of spirit to act in this vital life-enhancing way. Adults who themselves have been very discouraged or who have suffered from a deficit of praise in their lives often simply don't have enough of this generosity.

The Encouragers & The Rubbishers

You could discuss the following quotation:

> We all need love but who can do the loving?
>
> *(Oscar Wilde)*

... common feelings when having to live up to very high expectations of parents

> His love of his mother in the face of rejection at her hands…. is equivalent to discharging his love into an emotional vacuum…[he] feels reduced to a state of worthlessness, destitution or beggardom.
>
> *(Fairbairn 1940)*

If your teenager has parents like this, discuss the pressure and stress this can bring. Comment on how even for teenagers, just as for children, when parents are discouraging it can still feel like the whole world is discouraging. Encourage them to find adults in their life who are good at encouraging.

Specific Statements You Could Use

When people feel they are worthless it is often because others in their lives haven't been good at encouraging them and more often have been discouraging – sometimes because when they were children themselves, no one was good at encouraging them.

> I think people haven't done a good job at helping you to know how special you are.
>
> *(Hughes 2001)*

> When you're facing the gates of hell [discouragers] you've got your back to the gates of heaven [encouragers].
>
> *Anon*

> Schools are geared to helping pupils achieve good key stage and exam scores. They are not institutions created to help individual children to achieve their psychological growth.
>
> *(Feinstein 2000)*

The Encouragers & The Rubbishers

Activities for Development

Your Life as a Film Set

Ask the teenager to draw their life as a film set, showing themselves and the main characters in their life (both at home and at school). These are not necessarily the people they want to have in their life, for example, they might show a school bully.

Now ask them to draw themselves next to each of these people in terms of the size they feel when they are with that person.

If the teenager has drawn themselves as small – is this someone they need to spend less time with, and perhaps confront about how they are being treated, and then move away from them to people who make them stand tall!

Legacy of Shame

This exercise about childhood psychological messages and core beliefs will help the teenager to think further about the long-term effects of being discouraged, so that they can stand back and begin to separate the discourager from who they are.

Negative messages (either verbal or non-verbal) received in childhood can be particularly damaging as they occur at a time when both the sense of self and the social brain are still forming.

Read the list and tick any of the messages you think you were given as a child (these won't always have been said out loud) and the beliefs you hold about yourself as a result:

✴ Don't succeed   ✴ Don't be you (Don't Exist)

✴ Don't grow up   ✴ Don't make it

✴ Don't be important   ✴ Don't be a child

✴ Don't be someone in your own right   ✴ Don't

✴ Don't be   ✴ Don't think

Sometimes knowing this list (adapted from Berne 2009) can make teenagers re-think their core beliefs about themselves and give them more options to ensure such beliefs are not based on other's people's negativity.

Carrying Someone Else's Emotional Baggage

This exercise is about the inter-generational transmission of misery. When a parent has suffered considerable emotional pain, loss or trauma and doesn't get help to work through these feelings, their children and teenagers can be deeply affected.

Despite their very best efforts and intentions, the parent can pass on aspects of their own misery to their children. This can happen from generation to generation. It only takes one person to break the cycle, by getting some form of counselling or therapy through which the pain can be addressed and successfully modified. It can be enormously helpful for teenagers to separate out what is really true about themselves from how their negative view about themselves may have been heavily influenced by a parent's emotional baggage.

It can help, where appropriate, for the teenager to have a conversation with a parent about their emotional baggage. They may need help from you to find the right words to use.

✳ First, draw a quick sketch of two suitcases and label one 'My Parents' Emotional Baggage' and another one 'My Emotional Baggage'.

✳ Now fill the Parents' Suitcase with all the anxieties, traumas and unmourned losses that you think they are carrying around, e.g., 'Dad's father left home when he was four', 'Mum lost her first baby', 'Dad was badly bullied by his older brothers', 'Mum has a hang up about germs', 'Both parents fear of taking risks', 'Mum sometimes drinks too much'. It is fine to put both parents in the one suitcase!

✳ Look at what you have written. Consider which aspects of your parents' emotional baggage you think you have ended up carrying in your own life in some way (that is, the ones that affect you most). Write these in the suitcase entitled 'My Emotional Baggage'. Look at what you have written.

✳ Now draw a kite or balloon flying high – write on it the aspects of you that you think have not been affected by your parents' emotional baggage, e.g., your ability to take risks, your sense of calm, your courage, your generosity. Congratulate yourself on these.

✳ Finally, think how you could put down the baggage you are carrying which is a direct result of your parent's baggage.

Positive Generational Transfer

Ask the teenager to consider positive emotional inter-generational transmission. Ask them to draw or write down the good things that have been passed down to them from their parents (e.g., particular family traits or qualities).

Vital Psychology for the Practitioner

Common Underlying Causes

Consider if any of the following might fit with what you know of the teenager with whom you are working:

* Has adults in their life who don't know how vital encouragement is for a child and how this must be frequent and regular, with at least six praises for every one criticism.

* Has parents who have been unable to encourage the teenager as they have been too troubled to do so (through depression, anxiety, addiction to drugs or alcohol).

* Receive overtly spoken discouraging messages about making mistakes, needing to try harder, not being as good as their sibling.

* Parental messages were given in childhood about being stupid, worthless or clumsy.

* A general atmosphere where the child has picked up that they are often experienced as annoying, wearisome and irritating. (This can often be conveyed non-verbally.)

* Parents who demand very high standards in school assessments and other settings.

* Have been bullied and frequently subjected to cruel put-downs about themselves or members of their family, e.g. 'Your mum's a whore'.

* Had had teachers who are not good at encouragement.

What Life is Like for a Discouraged Teenager who Feels Unable to do Anything of Real Value

For discouraged teenagers, life can all too easily lose its magic, its fascination and its excitement. Each day can be met with dread of further accusations of inadequacy, failure and comments that they could do better.

The teenager who is discouraged can believe that all they do is lacking – anything they make, say, invent, write or dream of. When teenagers have suffered a lot of discouragement in their lives this can also lead to what is known as 'frustration avoidance', that is giving up very easily in the face of challenge or adversity.

This is in contrast to teenagers who have been encouraged, which brings with it energy enabling them to persevere and often triumph in the face of adversity.

Key Research on Self–Esteem in Teenagers

Feinstein, at the Centre for Economic Performance, assessed data on children aged ten collected through the 1970 British Cohort Study. Self-esteem was monitored. He then looked at what these children were earning when they were in their twenties. The data showed that self-esteem at aged ten was a very important indicator of high earnings in their twenties, far more than their academic ability (Feinstein 2000).

Negative Messages Given Before the Age of Six

Research shows that when children from birth to six years are given a diet of negative messages by a parent, it can be as powerful as hypnosis (Lipton 2011). The brain waves of children in this age group are often in a state that is known as 'low-frequency delta waves', the very same brain state as adults under hypnosis! So although it is a very dangerous time for receiving negative messages it is a very powerful time for positive ones. The child's sense of self is forming and when their brain waves are in this state it means they are very receptive (Laibow 2002).

The Damaging Nature of Shame

Some children and teenagers are disciplined through shame. Shame is a very powerful and painful emotion. It is experienced as an assault on the self. Guilt is arguably far easier to deal with as it is related to something you have done rather than your very personhood.

Shaming events can result in long-term negative core beliefs about the self as being worthless, rubbish, unimportant or intrinsically bad. Furthermore, when you have been shamed, there is always shame-based rage underneath, even if a teenager cuts off from this. This is extreme and intense, a direct response to the acute sense of assault from the shame. It is vital that shamed teenagers access this rage in order to find a boundary for transactions with potential shamers in the future.

The Long-Term Impact of Post-Natal Depression

'A deeper and more dreadful experience – the experience of the faceless mother, that is, the mother whose face does not light up at the sight of her child.' (Kohut 1979)

Some teenagers who have had a mother who was not helped during a period of post-natal depression may be still affected by this. If they don't know that their mother suffered in this way they will be unable to locate exactly an often deep sense of feeling worthless.

Research shows that post-natal depression (where the mother has been left unhelped) can really affect self-esteem in the teenage years, particularly with girls, even long after the mother is well again. Murray's research (1988) showed that if mothers were not helped with their post-natal depression, when their daughters hit their teenage years they too showed high levels of stress hormones. This makes them vulnerable to depression, anxiety or problems with anger.

Bibliography

Bar-Levav, R. (1988) *Thinking in the Shadow of Feelings*, Simon & Schuster, London.

Berne E. (2009) *Transactional Analysis in Psychotherapy*, Eigal Meirovich.

Fairbairn W.R.D. (1940) 'Schizoid Factors in the Personality' in *Psychoanalytic Studies of the Personality* (1952: 3–27) Tavistock/Routledge, London.

Feinstein L. (2000) 'The Relative Economic Importance of Academic, Psychological and Behavioural Attributes Developed in Childhood', Centre for Economic Performance, London.

Hughes D. (2001) Public Lecture 'Helping Children with Attachment Difficulties', The Centre for Child Mental Health, London.

Keenan B. (1992) *An Evil Cradling*, Vintage, London.

Kohut H. (1979) 'The Two Analyses of Mr Z', *International Journal of Psychoanalysis*, Vol. 60:3-27.

Laibow R.E. (1999-2000) *Biofeedback Health Inform's Resource Guide to Alternative Health*, Health Inform, Montrose NY.

Laibow R.E. (2002) Q-EEG Neurobiofeedback Treatment of Brain Injured Patients Part II, *J Neurotherapy*.

Lipton B. (2011) *The Biology of Belief: Unleashing the Power of Consciousness, Matter and Miracles*, Hay House Publishing, London.

Murray L. (1988) 'Effects of Postnatal Depression on Infant Development: Direct Studies of Early Mother-Infant Reactions', in Kumar R. & Brockington I.F. (eds), *Motherhood and Mental Illness 2: Causes and Consequences*, Wright, London/Boston.

Rowan J. (1986) *Ordinary Ecstasy: Humanistic Psychology in Action*, Routledge & Kegan Paul, London.

Sunderland M. (2003) *Helping Children with Low Self-Esteem*, Speechmark, Milton Keynes.

Me as a Walking Time-Bomb

For teenagers with poor impulse control who lash out when they are angry.

Objective

✳ To help the teenager learn when their anger is adaptive or maladaptive.

✳ To convey an understanding of the reptilian part of the brain (in terms of fight, flight, freeze) and to recognise when the alarm systems in their reptilian brain have been triggered.

✳ To develop calming capacities in the teenager.

✳ To provide the teenager with a coherent narrative and psychological understanding of why they might have problems with impulse control.

Me as a Walking Time-Bomb

Guidance for the Worksheet

You may find it useful to think about how your angry feelings often get you into trouble. It is possible to change this. You can think about your angry feelings in terms of your whole life, what you want for the rest of your life, what you might want to change or do differently.

It might help to think about this using some pictures. Have a look at the pictures on the worksheet and their captions. If any of the pictures or captions describe how you feel now or have felt in the past, maybe when you were still a child, please tick the box or colour in the picture. If none of the pictures describe what you have felt or feel now when you get really angry, draw or write what how it feels in the empty box.

Me as a Walking Time-Bomb

When I get angry I sometimes feel

On fire

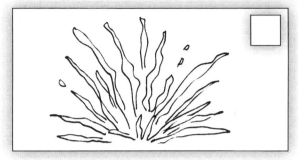

Like an earthquake inside me

Like a flood inside me

A bomb

A monster

A scream that can't stop screaming

A wall of hate

A tornado

A war inside me

What to Say to the Teenager

It will be useful to have a basic diagram of the brain on hand showing the prefrontal cortex and the reptilian brain.

As you hold your discussion, show the teenager which area of the brain you are talking about.

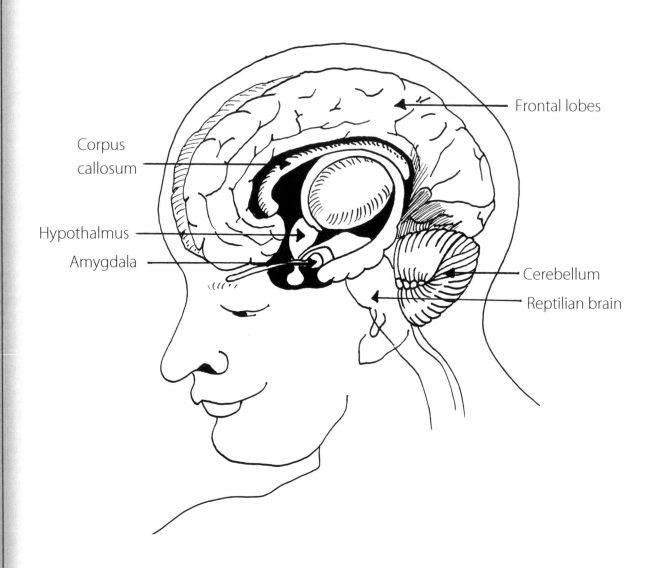

Corpus callosum

Hypothalmus

Amygdala

Frontal lobes

Cerebellum

Reptilian brain

Talk About ...

... angry outbursts being modelled on the behaviour of angry parents

Some teenagers who lash out in anger find it difficult not to do so. Often this comes from years of a parent modelling this way of dealing with anger. This goes hand-in-hand with little or no modelling of anger being resolved through thoughtful words. It is all too easy for teenagers to do what they have seen their parents doing.

The following quotation from a teenager could be a valuable starting point for a discussion:

> My dad's never hit my mum but he's grabbed her, he's grabbed her by the throat and stuff like that … And I can remember going back, when I was arguing with my mum at the bus stop in town and I was arguing with her and I grabbed her by the throat … I could see like my dad in me then and that was scary. I didn't like that, yeah.'
>
> *(Barter et al 2009)*

... the origins of emotional dysregulation and what it feels like to live with it

Some people find it hard not to lash out when they are angry, because their parents didn't help them with *their* anger when they were children.

Whenever a child has an intense feeling such as anger or distress, they are what is known as 'emotionally dysregulated'. This means that they are in such a state that stress hormones flood through their brain and body, resulting in a very poor ability to think and an impulse to fight, flight or freeze. In other words the way they think is geared to threat levels.

When their parent soothes, calms and understands them, the child's brain and body calm dramatically, the stress hormones return to base rate and they can function again. The parent's empathic listening enables the child to move back to a state of emotional regulation and a feeling of well-being. The more this happens throughout their childhood, the more new brain pathways form in the child's prefrontal cortex (the higher, 'human', thinking brain). Some of these pathways, known as top-down brain pathways, will naturally inhibit the primitive fight, flight, freeze impulses in the reptilian part of the brain.

Me as a Walking Time-Bomb

... what makes a parent an effective emotional regulator

For a parent or other adult to be an emotional regulator for a child, they need to be able to find the space in their own minds to think into and feel the child's pain. When parents do this over time, the child develops systems in their own brain which enable them to manage stress well and not to blow when someone really winds them up.

Some parents don't have any space in their minds to do this, due to being full of their own problems and emotional pain. So if parents are angry, anxious or feeling really low it can be very difficult to be an emotional regulator. In these cases the child doesn't develop the stress-regulating functions in their brain and sometimes worse. The child can end up discharging the tension from their parent's painful feelings or the painful feelings in the parental relationship, as well as their own raw feelings. As one child who had a very angry dad said, 'It is difficult to have my feelings when daddy is having his all the time'. A child's behaviour is often a barometer of their parent's emotional state, parental stress, or the parent's brushed-under-the-carpet feelings and the emotional atmosphere in the home.

It is as if the child feels as follows, which is a major cause of their challenging behaviour:

✳ I can't regulate my rage because no one helped me do that.

✳ I can't regulate my emotions because no one helped me do that.

✳ I can't reflect on my feelings, because no one helped me do that.

✳ I have no sense of self because no one helped me to form that.

The great thing is that it is never too late to develop these stress-calming systems. If you talk about your feelings to someone who can really listen and understand, then you too can develop these vital systems in the brain.

Activities for Development

Anger as Emotional Baggage

Ask the teenager to discuss the following quotation:

> Anger is like raw garbage – banana peels, chicken bones, old brown lettuce. If you don't deal with it, you add to the pile, and over the years it loses its form and turns into sludge, until you no longer can say "I am angry because this or that happened". You're left with brown yucky stuff without anything in it that you can name.
>
> *(Blume 1990)*

Ask the teenager to think about any emotional baggage that they might be carrying and haven't addressed.

Suggest that they draw what it feels like to carry it.

Ask them to imagine how it feels – does it feel like baggage, a weight on their shoulders, a heavy heart, carrying other people's baggage?

Now ask them to draw their emotional baggage and encourage them to think of words or images to write on their picture.

Ask them how long they've been carrying the baggage and whether anyone has ever helped them with it.

The Good & Bad Things about Anger and Rage

Look at the picture on the worksheet.

Colour in or circle the images and words that describe what you think about your anger.

Now you have done this, is there anything you would like to change in terms of how you express your angry feelings?

The Good & Bad Things about Anger and Rage

Vital Psychology for the Practitioner

The Stress Regulatory Systems in the Brain

As discussed above, many teenagers lash out in anger because they have not developed stress regulatory systems in their brains. By and large their parent is not getting enough support or help with their own feelings, so they are not able to function as a psycho-biochemical regulator. This often leaves the child in a state of unsoothed stress.

The brain habituates to these states and, as the affective neuroscientists say, 'States become Traits'. Many teenagers who lash out when angry are just like toddlers and indeed for some their brain development is still at the stage of a toddler. When a child lives day-in, day-out with bodily and biochemical states of hyper-arousal, resulting from a parent shouting, being angry, or suffering from anxiety or depression, it is no wonder that that the intensity of their feeling must be discharged.

However, when you help the teenager to talk about their feelings, and in your presence, to feel them in their full intensity, your empathy, calmness and containment will help to develop the stress regulatory systems. These include top-down brain pathways (Cozolino 2002) from the higher brain to the lower parts of the brain – which naturally inhibit primitive impulses for fight, flight and freeze.

Fear and Hope

Some teenagers are very frightened by the intensity of their anger and need to speak about that fear. They can be reassured if they know that it is common for people to be frightened of their level of anger. They can be told that it is possible for them to change brain pathways and brain biochemical states so that they no longer need to feel so unsafe about themselves.

Why Anger Seems to Offer so Much to Some Teenagers

It is important to talk with teenager about what anger offers them. It can be rather like a drug, as for some teenagers its rewards are great. Until these are understood and acknowledged it can be very difficult to change.

Some of the common rewards are as follows:

1 Anger can protect you from painful feelings. It can be much easier to feel anger than many other feelings. So teenagers get angry instead of letting themselves know that what they are really feeling is pain about awful things that have happened in their lives.

2 There is an adrenaline rush in the brain and body from anger. It can make you feel powerful, very alive, excited. So if you are feeling small, and shut down emotionally, anger can be like a great drug that takes you out of your painful emotional states. It is not hard to see stealing, lying, and smashing things up as just one step further on from this.

3 Anger can give the teenager an identity, a sense of who they are. As Barrows remarks about a teenager he was working with, 'I thought he was afraid that if he stopped his cruelty and noisy games, he'd be too empty handed.' (2003)

'Love made Angry' & 'Love made Hungry'

For some teenagers, the self-awareness that will enable them to shift out of persistent, primitive angry states will involve a conversation about the people who matter or who have mattered to them. Often their first love is their mum or their dad. When a teenager has known painful rejection, they can become very angry or emotionally very hungry. The former can manifest in a generally angry attitude towards people and life in general. The latter shows itself in clingy, needy behaviour, particularly in intimate relationships. The teenager with 'love made hungry' (Guntrip 1969) can often get desperately jealous. They often 'need' their partner to make up for lack of love or empathic attention in childhood. Love made angry or hungry can also result from the child having experienced long periods of separation from an attachment figure during childhood.

Angry Outbursts that are Shame-Rage

Teenagers who exhibit angry outbursts can usefully discuss whether their anger is shame-based. This is anger that has resulted from past experiences of humiliating abuses of power where the teenager is made to feel worthless, useless and unworthy of respect. Shameful experiences such as these leave a seething undercurrent of rage. This can be released at any time and is often first released during the teenage years with the build-up of hormonal forces to fuel it. Being shamed always need to be spoken and raged about and grieved over. If this doesn't happen it can carry a lethal power into relationships again and again.

Appropriate & Inappropriate Anger

This is a useful discussion with the teenager, particularly when he or she has not had good role models in their life regarding healthy anger. You could start the discussion as follows:

'Sometimes, anger may be an appropriate to a situation – perhaps when someone is trying to shame or bully you. Saying a clear "No" or something like "I won't let you shame me" or "Enough", is using anger as a vital boundary-setting emotion. At other times anger is not appropriate. Instead it is a destructive over-reaction. As Aristotle said, "Being angry is easy. It's knowing when, where, how, in what intensity and with whom to be angry, that takes intelligence".'

Bibliography

Barrows P.S. (ed.) (2003) *Key Papers from the Journal of Child Psychotherapy*, Brunner-Routledge, London.

Barter C., McCarry M., Berridge D. & Evans K. (2009) *Partner exploitation and violence in teenage intimate relationships*, University of Bristol & NSPCC, nspcc.org.uk.

Blume E.S. (1990) *Secret Survivors: Uncovering Incest and its Aftereffects in Women*, John Wiley, Chichester/New York.

Cozolino L.J. (2002) *The Neuroscience of Psychotherapy: Building and Rebuilding the Human Remain*, W.W. Norton & Co., London

Guntrip H. (1969) *Schizoid Phenomena, Object-Relations and the Self*, Hogarth, London.

Dog Eat Dog

For teenagers who are angry because they have been treated with cruelty.

Objective

✳ To help the teenager to be able to trust the practitioner enough to talk about the painful events in their life.

✳ To enable teenagers who are perpetrators of cruelty to talk about how they were abused as children and may still be in the present.

✳ To enable teenagers who are perpetrators of abuse to be able to feel again. This means that they will feel pain at the pain of others (being distress averse) rather than continue to be distress excited (get a thrill out of hurting others).

✳ To gain awareness and psychological knowledge about why they are sometimes cruel.

Dog Eat Dog

Guidance for the Worksheet

When you've known too much cruelty, hurt and attack in your life, it is easy to think that it is a 'Dog Eat Dog' world. In such a world, you might find yourself being hateful or cruel to someone else. Perhaps this is how you were treated, so it feels normal to you. Perhaps you feel justified in causing hurting, because of what that person has done to you. Perhaps it gives you a real power buzz. But maybe a part of you feels uncomfortable about it on some level. Perhaps on some level you don't like yourself for doing it.

You may find it useful to think about what makes you see this world as a 'Dog Eat Dog' place, particularly in terms of what you want for the rest of your life, what you might want to change or do differently.

It might help to think about this using some pictures. Have a look at the pictures and captions on the worksheet.

If any of the pictures or captions describes how you feel or how you have felt in the past, maybe when you were just a child, tick the box on the picture or colour the picture in. If none of the pictures describe what you have felt or feel now, draw or write in the empty box what you feel inside when you feel like it is a 'Dog Eat Dog' world.

Dog Eat Dog

I steal, lie, smash, hurt. It's about surviving.

Constantly seen as bad/to blame for bad things that happen.

I live in a world without kindness.

Fed up with other people's crazy stuff.

Like I've got no place in this lousy world.

Just had too much abuse in my life.

What to Say to the Teenager

Use the table entitled 'Why Teenagers are Cruel and Cause Hurt' for material which you feel is relevant for a deeper conversation with the teenager about feeling they live in a 'Dog Eat Dog' world.

WHY TEENAGERS ARE CRUEL AND CAUSE HURT	
Cruelty when something in the here and now triggers childhood feelings or being hurt, shamed or humiliated.	Any experience in the teenage years which is perceived as being rejected, attacking or disrespectful can trigger childhood feelings of being hurt, shamed or humiliated. The teenager then attacks the person they perceive as causing hurting. Hence the well-known scenario of a massive over-reaction when a teenager thinks someone is looking at them with disrespect, 'He was dissing me.' This can be enough to beat someone up. The teenager is not aware that their perception in the present is fuelled by the pain of their past – and so the attack and cruelty can feel justified. With unprocessed childhood pain, there can also be an accompanying sense of 'I will not let you make me feel like that again – so I will attack you' and 'I'll make *you* feel what people have made *me* feel', i.e., rubbish, useless, scum.
Cruelty because when the teenager felt their love was rejected, loving turned to hating.	The child who feels they have lost their mother's or father's love (perhaps to a new baby or to an alcohol addiction), can kill off their own love as it is too painful. They move into hating instead. Loving made the child feel terrible, vulnerable and impotent. Hate makes them feel strong, invincible and powerful. 'Human beings all prefer to be bad and strong rather than weak.' (Guntrip 1969)

WHY TEENAGERS ARE CRUEL AND CAUSE HURT

Cruelty resulting from needing to make others feel the complete helplessness felt in childhood.	When a baby is left in a state of distress by an emotionally unresponsive parent it can lead to feelings of terrifying helplessness. Winnicott (1965) refers to such states in the baby as primitive agonies – feelings of falling forever, dying and/or dying repeatedly or falling apart. We know that infants can cut off from such pain, but the memory of the pain doesn't go away. It lives on as a traumatic memory. We know that traumatic memories very often get played out in the form of re-victimisation (causing someone else to feel what you felt). Bullying is often an attack on the vulnerability and helplessness in others that has been killed off in oneself. For example, Bowlby (1978) found that toddlers who had been left to cry as babies, in turn hit babies in a nursery when they cried. We also know that the key contributor of whether a person develops post-traumatic stress disorder is their experiencing a state of helplessness during the painful event. A very common defence against helplessness is for someone to become dominant in the future, a bully or abuser of some sort, 'I will be the powerful one and make you the helpless one this time round'. As Horney (1977) says, 'When he defeats others he wins a triumphant elation which obscures his own hopeless defeat'.
Cruelty resulting from a childhood environment devoid of empathy, kindness or concern.	A parent who is unable to empathise with or register their child's distress or emotional pain, leaves that child, in their teenage years, similarly unable to feel pain at the pain of others. Empathy is one of the main inhibitors of cruel unkind acts. Hence Batmanghelidjh's observation (2009) 'Cruel or violent teenagers don't need punishment – it won't work (there is an 87 percent rate of re-offending in youth criminal justice system) … Often their punishment is nothing compared to the abusive acts they have experienced. What they need is to be helped to feel again.'

Dog Eat Dog

WHY TEENAGERS ARE CRUEL AND CAUSE HURT

Cruelty resulting from family relationships being mostly about power and control over others.	These teenagers have witnessed and been on the receiving end of too many 'power over' interactions in the home (e.g., criticism, commands, put-downs, and not warmth, gentleness and child-led play). This can lead to the internalising of negative relationship patterns, so that their own peer relationships are simply variations on the theme of submission and dominance. The teenager dominates, attacks or criticises as they themselves have been treated. In other words they internalise negative and controlling relational patterns and play them out on others, described as RIGS (representations of interactions that have been generalised (Stern 1985). Furthermore, teenagers who persistently engage in destructive or abusive patterns in relationships often have no 'RIGS' of love, compassion or co-operation.
Over-strict discipline.	Being shamed and humiliated in the name of discipline (often because parents have no notion of how to do it differently) provokes feelings of rage and hate. However, it is usually felt to be far too dangerous to become angry with the disciplining parent as this may provoke even more attack, so the rage and hate are forced 'underground'. These are then redirected at and focused on someone else. (This pattern of doing to others what has been done to you very often happens outside of awareness.) The teenager has lived in an atmosphere of criticism, i.e., 'You are bad for doing this terrible thing and need to be punished', rather than 'It's not OK you did this and the consequences will be this, but let me try to understand the feelings that led you to do it'.
Childhood trauma.	In Post-Traumatic Stress Disorder (PTSD), there is often a need to replay the trauma in some form, as the mind attempts to come to terms with the experience (it can be replayed through flashbacks, nightmares or *re-enactment* in real life). However, often in the replaying, this time round the traumatised person takes the role of the persecutor and someone else is the victim. The abused child may become an abuser in their own right in adulthood, often clearly replicating the type of abuse that they suffered themselves.

Dog Eat Dog

WHY TEENAGERS ARE CRUEL AND CAUSE HURT	
Childhood abuse.	Experience of sexual or physical abuse often includes a whole host of factors which, if not addressed, can easily lead to troubled behaviour in later life. To be specific, childhood abuse often results in a need to keep the abusing parent good by repressing and transferring feelings of rage and hate on to others. So patterns of submission/dominance are established particularly in the teenager's partner relationships or as bullying in the school or community environment.
Self-hate (because parents were not good at loving).	Self-hate as a result of a harsh childhood can be displaced on to someone else, as it is too painful to endure. So another person or group becomes a projection of the teenager's own hated self. In other words, contemptuous attacks on the self are turned outwards and become hateful attacks of others, who are found to be 'pathetic', 'puny', 'stupid'. In the extreme, this is why some murders can so easily have been suicides. In short, 'I hate you and want to hurt you because you are a projection of my own hated self'. When someone devalues the self-hating teenager, calls them 'slut', 'scum', or treats them as rubbish, it can trigger intolerable feelings of feeling worthless and shame. The teenager's cruel retaliation is a way of protecting themselves from re-triggering childhood feelings of an unbearable assault on the self. Self-esteem can be so painfully low that any criticism feels like a mortal blow. 'Returning' the attack can feel like the best form of defence, so others are put down in shaming and deeply hurtful ways. This is attack as self-preservation, 'I feel so bad about myself, I want to make you feel bad instead of me' (again this process is outside of conscious awareness).

Dog Eat Dog

WHY TEENAGERS ARE CRUEL AND CAUSE HURT	
Communication of unbearable childhood feelings 'by impact'.	Communication by impact (Casement 1985) is an out of awareness action fuelled by a desire to '*make* you know what I am feeling by making *you* feel it'. So, for example, I will call you all manner of derogatory names to convey to you what it felt like for me to be treated as useless or rubbish. Tragically, this unconscious communication usually only gets read to the point where it can be understood and resolved if the teenager has access to a counsellor or therapist. The therapist responds to the 'communication by impact' in such a way as to convey: 'You want to let me know about what you feel, by making me feel it, and through empathising with you, I will let you know that your message has been received and understood'. But of course, it is not the job of the police to either read crimes as communications, or to respond to such communications with empathy.

Talk About...

... how cruelty breeds cruelty

Use the table entitled 'Why Teenagers are Cruel and Cause Hurt' as a starting point for your discussion on sources of cruelty.

... the key reasons why people are cruel to others

No one is born cruel. If a child doesn't receive enough love, kindness and human warmth and does experience too many adults being harsh or cruel, they can all too easily become cruel themselves. Following are some of the key reasons why people are cruel. Ask the teenager which, if any, of the following factors they think have lead them to be cruel.

✳ Cruelty when something in the here and now triggers childhood feelings of being hurt, shamed or humiliated.
✳ Cruelty because when he felt his love was rejected, loving turned to hating.
✳ Cruelty resulting from needing to make others feel the utter helplessness he has felt in childhood.
✳ Cruelty resulting from a childhood environment devoid of empathy, kindness or concern.
✳ Cruelty resulting from family relationships being mostly about power over and control.
✳ Over-strict discipline.
✳ Childhood trauma/abuse.
✳ Self-hate (because of having parents who weren't good at loving).

Dog Eat Dog

… how teenagers can be cruel because the only relationships they have known are all about power and control

Some people are cruel because they have known too little kindness in their lives. Their parents were harsh, cold, angry or unavailable for too much of the time. Teenagers who are cruel more than anything need empathy and understanding for the cruelty they themselves have received.

> Cruel or violent teenagers don't need punishment - it won't work (there is an 87 percent rate of re-offending in youth criminal justice system) … Often their punishment is nothing compared to the abusive acts they have experienced. What they need is to be helped to feel again.
>
> *(Batmanghelidjh 2009)*

… what teenagers said when asked why they abused their partners

✳ To hurt them

✳ To impress others

✳ To get what I wanted

✳ To humiliate them

✳ I was just messing around

(Barter et al 2009)

Quotations for Discussion

> Human beings all prefer to be bad and strong rather than weak.
>
> *(Guntrip 1969)*

> When he defeats others he wins a triumphant elation which obscures his own hopeless defeat.
>
> *(Horney 1977)*

> Young people who view physical violence as 'only joking' or messing around will have little motivation to stop, irrespective of its consequences.
>
> *(Sears et al 2006)*

Exercises for Development

The Cruel and the Kind

Use a sand play box divided into two or a piece of paper with a line down the middle. On one side draw, write or use sand play images to present the kindness and human warmth you have received in your life. On the other side draw, write or use sand play images to present the cruelty and coldness you have received in your life. When you stand back and look at what you had done – what does it make you feel. How might you want to change things in your future?

Vital Psychology for the Practitioner

The vital information for the practitioner in this section has been provided in table form (see 'Why Teenagers are Cruel and Cause Hurt' table above), however the following considerations are offered in addition.

The tough defended teenager who is cruel to others needs empathy for the pain they have suffered in their life. Until they feel another's pain at their pain it will be difficult for them to let go of their defences in order to feel again.

If we just write off murderers, rapists and criminals as bad or evil, we don't need to reflect on their childhood experiences of humiliation, rejection, feeling profoundly unloved/undervalued. As Hyatt Williams (a psychoanalyst who worked in prisons) states (1998), wherever there has been a murder there has been a soul murder, or actual murderous attack on the perpetrator when he or she was a child. We have only compassion for those who are badly abused as babies or children, but if they grow up and act out on others what has happened to them (communication by impact), they are despised.

Because of childhood abuse and trauma, relational events such as an adult engaging the teenager in a therapeutic conversation can be met with mistrust. Hyper-vigilance for any possibility of threat means that warmth and kindness are often not registered. This can be very disheartening for the practitioner. However, if you stick with the teenager and empathise, and even engage them in conversations about trust and mistrust, they will at some point let you in.

Dog Eat Dog

Bibliography

Barter C., McCarry M., Berridge D. & Evans K. (2009) *Partner exploitation and violence in teenage intimate relationships*, University of Bristol & NSPCC, nspcc.org.uk.

Bowlby J. (1978) *Attachment and Loss: Volume 3 – Loss, Sadness and Depression*, Penguin, Harmondsworth.

Guntrip H. (1969) *Schizoid Phenomena, Object-Relations and the Self*, Hogarth, London.

Horney K. (1977) *The Neurotic Personality of Our Time*, Routledge, London.

Hyatt Williams A. (1998) *Cruelty, Violence and Murder: Understanding the Criminal Mind (Library of Object Relations)*, Jason Aranson, London.

Sears H., Byers S., Whelan J. & Saint-Pierre G. (2006) 'If it hurts you, then it is not a joke, Adolescents' ideas and experiences of abusive behaviour in dating relationships', *Journal of Interpersonal Violence*, Vol. 21(9): 191–207.

Stern D.N. (1985) *The Interpersonal World of the Infant*, Basic Books, New York.

Winnicott D.W. (1965) *The Maturational Process and the Facilitating Environment*, Hogarth, London.

Dog Eat Dog

Haunted by Bad Stuff from the Past

For teenagers who are aware that their anger is sometimes over the top because of painful life experiences.

Objective

This exercise aims to help teenagers to distinguish their here-and-now anger from anger bottled up inside due to painful past experiences (emotional-baggage anger). Such feelings do not just go away, however much they are denied. As Freud said, they just 'proliferate in the dark'. It is helpful to explain to teenagers some key points regarding anger from the past, in particular the following:

Emotional-baggage anger …

✳ … is anger that is being expressed to someone in the present, which really belongs to someone in your past, often a parent figure.

✳ … feels primitive and intense because it is unworked-through and the years of being stored up inside you have just added to its intensity.

✳ … is usually identified by the intensity and volume of your reaction.

✳ … is so strong that it often destroys the important relationships you have.

Haunted by Bad Stuff from the Past

Guidance for the Worksheet

If you feel rage when someone doesn't listen to you, nags you, tells you how you are failing in some way, rather than just irritation, then you may be experiencing emotional-baggage anger. This means you have anger bottled up inside you from painful experiences in the past.

Now think of a more recent painful argument or angry outburst that you can remember clearly. Have a look at the statements in the two tables on the worksheet. Tick any of the boxes that describe how you felt when you were angry. Now look at the table with the most ticks. This should help to inform you whether during this incident, most of your anger came from pain in your past, played out in the present or whether it was healthy here-and-now anger.

If your anger is mainly from past pain (emotional-baggage anger), talk through the memories that you think are fuelling your painful angry outbursts.

When I got angry recently I felt ...

EMOTIONAL-BAGGAGE ANGER	
Huge intense feeling. The event has triggered feelings of hurt, rage and shame or feelings of betrayal from your past.	
A preoccupation with revenge. You have a strong desire to make the other person feel what they have made you feel, or worse.	
A desire to hurt. You have a desire to hurt with actions and/or words.	
Angry, indignant or hate-filled thoughts keep going round and round in your head. You are preoccupied by what happened, and can't seem to let it go and move on.	
Kept having an in-depth post-mortem examination of the event. You keep thinking about what you said and did, and what you could have said or done.	
Had negative responses to apologies or attempts by the other person to make amends. This is because you want to punish and not resolve. You are punishing this person for old hurts from people in your past.	
An underlying deep sense of hurt. Beneath all the anger or rage, a deep hurt has been re-triggered from relationships in your past e.g., not being responded to, being rejected, discouraged, being shamed or humiliated, not being understood.	
Relief at having a core belief about yourself or others confirmed. For example you felt, 'See, this proves how unlovable I am', 'See, this proves that you can't ever really trust anyone', 'See, this proves that everyone is really out to get you.'	

Haunted by Bad Stuff from the Past

When I got angry recently I felt ...

HERE-AND-NOW ANGER	
The focus is on the resolution of the problem not on the desire to hurt. 'We have a problem, a difference of opinion here, so how can we resolve it?' This is completely different in tone and energy from a feeling of 'You are to blame because...' or 'It's all your fault.'	
The anger is vibrant and then soon over. Some people call this 'warm anger'. There is a 'clean' feel to it, although it can still be loud and passionate.	
You see the person you are angry with as annoying, irritating or frustrating. The offending other person makes you angry, frustrated and very annoyed, rather than the extremes of emotional-baggage anger where the offending other person is seen as evil, an abuser or a psychopath.	
You don't want revenge, just to sort things out. This is in contrast to the vindictiveness and/or fantasies of wanting to hurt or destroy of emotional-baggage anger.	
Healthy anger is short-lived, communicated clearly and effectively and so you can move on. Once you've said what you are angry about, and you feel heard and understood by the other person, you feel better.	
Rows, conflicts and arguments do not feel like catastrophic or dangerous events, just a normal part of life. You know that you can express anger in ways that leave the other person OK. You do not use blame or insults. Your language says '*I feel* angry' rather than '*You are* bad'.	
Healthy anger leaves you feeling OK about yourself and the other person soon afterwards. You accept any apologies given and are able to talk about how you may have contributed to the situation. You genuinely try to listen and understand the other person's point of view.	

Useful exercise as development

Foresight, Mid-sight, Hindsight

Discuss with the teenager how on future occasions they could better support themselves by informing a trusted friend or other person when they think they might move or have moved into Emotional Baggage Anger. The concepts of foresight, mid-sight and hindsight can be very helpful here.

Foresight: 'What I am going to say might seem somewhat irrational, because I think this whole issue has triggered a painful memory for me.' This alerts the other person to the fact that there may be a lot of childhood rage and hurt coming their way, and not to take it all personally.

Mid-sight: 'Hey, I'm sorry. I think I'm shouting now because I seem to have triggered into something here, which is probably nothing to do with you.'

Hindsight: 'Look, I've come to say I'm sorry. When I thought about what I said to you, I felt awful. I was being over the top. I think what I said to you wasn't actually about you. It was my angry feelings towards my mother for leaving me.'

Of course, foresight is best, but mid-sight is also very socially intelligent and hindsight can heal a lot in a relationship too.

Vital psychology for the practitioner

In a longitudinal study Hauser (2006) and his colleagues interviewed a number of teenagers and asked them to speak about their lives. The teenagers had all done awful things, some had even committed murder.

Hauser followed these teenagers up when they were thirty years of age. The people who were doing well were distinguished from the ones who were doing badly by several key factors including self-awareness and the capacity to reflect. They were interested in psychological experiences and the process of relationships. They paid attention to how they behaved with other people. The ones not doing well had no such interests. According to Hauser, 'All of the kids are impulsive at times. But the resilient ones also give their lives and problems steady and serious attention.'

It seems clear that if we help teenagers to reflect in ways such as those described in these exercises and their accompanying psychological knowledge, teenagers can develop self-awareness. As Hauser found, this is absolutely key to enabling troubled teenagers to make that vital shift from destructive behaviour with the potential to ruin their lives, to being able to thrive.

Bibliography

Hauser S.T., Allen J.P. & Golden E. (2006) *Out of the Woods: Tales of Resilient Teens*, Harvard University Press, London/Cambridge, MA.